Nature in Mind

Nature in Mind explores a kind of madness at the core of the developed world that has separated the growth of human cultural systems from the destruction of the environment on which these systems depend. It is now becoming increasingly clear that the contemporary Western lifestyle not only has a negative impact on the ecosystems of the earth but also has a detrimental effect on human health and psychological wellbeing. The book compares the work of Gregory Bateson and Henry Corbin and shows how an understanding of the "imaginal world" within the practice of systemic psychotherapy and ecopsychology could provide a language shared by both nature and mind. This book argues the case for bringing nature-based work into mainstream education and therapy practice. It is an invitation to radically reimagine the relationship between humans and nature and provides a practical and epistemological guide to reconnecting human thinking with the ecosystems of the earth.

Roger Duncan is a registered Systemic Psychotherapist who works with children and adolescents in the NHS and in private practice with individuals, families, and organizations.

Nature in Mind

Systemic Thinking and Imagination in Ecopsychology and Mental Health

Roger Duncan

Routledge
Taylor & Francis Group

LONDON AND NEW YORK

First published 2018
by Routledge
2 Park Square, Milton Park, Abingdon, Oxon OX14 4RN

and by Routledge
711 Third Avenue, New York, NY 10017

Routledge is an imprint of the Taylor & Francis Group, an informa business

British Library Cataloguing-in-Publication Data
A catalogue record for this book is available from the British Library

Library of Congress Cataloging-in-Publication Data
A catalog record has been requested for this book

ISBN: 978-1-78220-377-3 (pbk)

Typeset in Times New Roman
by Apex CoVantage, LLC

This book is dedicated to my children Aurora, Esme, and Josh for all they have taught me and to my wife Joanna for her support and belief in the integrity of my long journey to write this book.
With gratitude to Val and Pete, my adoptive parents and Bill and Barb, my birth parents.

Contents

Acknowledgements

This book would not have been written without the contribution of a wealth of personal experiences and encounters that need acknowledgement. Firstly a deep and heartfelt thanks to the many people, from different tribal groups, that I met on my travels who offered me food, shelter, and showed me hospitality and humanity. To my teachers and fellow students of Waldorf Education for long discussions on what Rudolf Steiner was really trying to communicate. These included; Alan Hall, the late Steven Edelglass, Yvan Rioux, and Dr. James Dyson amongst others.

I'm grateful to Aonghus Gordon, founder of Ruskin Mill Trust for the opportunity to put some of Steiner's ideas into practice. I'm also grateful to fellow staff of Ruskin Mill for the years of practical work, play, and discussion in our work with an extraordinary group of students. These staff included, my wife Joanna, Rich Pirie, Lucy Meikle, Arian Leljak, Jonathan Code, Rich Turley, Alun Hughes, Caro Birtles, Michael and Linda Frosch, Julian Pyzer, Iona Fredenburgh, Kelvin Hall, and so many more people I had contact with for those eighteen years.

I would like to thank Julian Thomson, Ginny Moore, Dr. Will James, Rich Turley, Alun Hughes, Richard Macbeth, and Rich Pirie for their help in building and establishing the wilderness experience work. Thanks also to Caroline Pakel, Ed Berger, Micheil Gordon and Tom Fox.

I would also like to thank David Wendl-Berry for introducing me to vision quest and the work of The School of Lost Borders and to Pippa Bondy, Lucy Voelcker and Jeremy Thres for our conversations and our work together.

I owe a deep debt of gratitude to Meredith Little and the late Steven Foster founders of The School of Lost Borders who learnt from an indigenous lineage how to part the veil that separates nature and the human psyche and then, with deep humility, gave this experience back to people who had lost it.

I would like to thank the teachers on my Systemic Family Therapy training, Jacqui Sayers and Mark Rivett for support and guidance in my training and in helping me to make links between Bateson's work and ecopsychology. I would also like to thank Dr. Jeremy Woodcock, Philip Trenchard, and Jinny Paige Cook who played significant parts in my decision to train as a Systemic Family Therapist. I would also like to thank David Slattery for his patience and guidance in deepening my understanding of relationships within my personal journey.

Finally, I am deeply grateful to Dr. Lorraine Fish for her support in editing and proofreading this book, and her guidance and knowledge of how and where this work connects to the academic field of ecopsychology.

About the author

Roger Duncan trained as a biologist, Waldorf teacher, and wilderness rites of passage guide with The School of Lost Borders before becoming a Systemic Family Therapist and has been involved in nature-based practice for thirty years. He was one of the pioneer tutors of Ruskin Mill Education Trust, developing therapeutic education programmes for complex adolescents in the woodlands and wilderness settings and had a leadership role in senior management. He currently works as a Systemic Family Therapist in the NHS and in private practice, with individuals, families, and organizations. His intention is to find innovative ways to bring experiential encounters with the imaginal world into mainstream culture.

Introduction

What's the problem?

It sometimes seems that human culture is sleep walking into a series of ever-deeper humanitarian and environmental disasters, and even with the increased environmental awareness and wide spread social education, the future does not look hopeful. In fact, it looks unlikely that much of human culture and the ecosystems we have learnt to love will immerge intact from this process of catastrophic change. Despite increasingly complex technological developments this process of environmental degradation seems difficult to stop.

However, in 1988 British documentary film maker Alan Ereira was contacted by one of the last indigenous pre-Columbian South American tribes, called the Kogi. The Kogi had managed to evade conquest by the Spanish by retreating high into the Sierra Nevada Mountains of Columbia. Here they were able to keep their indigenous culture intact by isolating themselves from Western cultures. Through the training of shamans called mamas they believed they could communicate with the earth. According to the Kogi this initiation process involved mamas being identified at birth and then removed from their family at seven months old and kept in a darkened initiation lodge and were only allowed out for a short period at night, until they reached adolescence. During this process they were slowly taught how to communicate with nature, through a particular type of thinking. They also learnt cosmological stories that described the complex systemic relationship between human beings, nature, and the cosmos. After this initiation the mamas believed that they were able to read nature in a way that supported the ecological integration of their culture. The Kogi believed that it was their role to take care of the earth, and without their daily shamanic practices the earth would begin to die.

The Kogi contacted Alan because they had observed the reduced snow on the Sierra Nevada Mountains and understood that the earth's climate was changing. This, they believed, was the result of the activities of Western cultures, because they were not able to understand or communicate with the earth. The Kogi hoped that by making a film about this, Western cultures (who they called the younger brothers) would understand the complex and interconnected quality of the ecosystems and change their destructive practices. If this did not happen, then the Kogi believed the world would see an increase in uncontrollable diseases, flooding, and other climactic events, as the earth tried to shed itself of humanity in a process of systemic self-healing.

Twenty-eight years later in 2016, professor of psychiatry Daniel Siegel challenged the Western medical model of the mind and suggested that mind is an emergent and systemic phenomenon that connects individuals and the planet. Siegel proposed, like the Kogi shamans, that a mechanistic approach is not only leading to the destruction of the planet but is also insufficient to describe the complexities of mental health (Siegel, 2017).

The urgency of global catastrophe is real, but it is never too late for systems to change, in fact, change is intrinsic to the very nature of systems. The earth has been through catastrophic systemic environmental changes before and will do so again. It is our current human civilization that is not prepared or ready for this inevitable transformation. The threads of a new way of thinking and working already exist in our culture, if we know where to look for them and the work of reconnecting these threads is loosely linked to the emerging discipline of ecopsychology, or nature based practice, and sometimes just called "the work".

This book is therefore about connecting disciplines to create consilience, a coming together, in order to understand the relationship between humans and nature in a new way. This process of reconnecting with a deeper understanding of nature has been influenced by a small group of highly original thinkers, who have described the process in detail. They include amongst others: Carl Jung, Henry Corbin, James Hillman, Gregory Bateson, and Rudolf Steiner, all of whom point to a different way of seeing the world that is non-reductionist, complex, systemic, and essentially healthier, and characterized by an emergent spiritually.

This book is also about re-envisioning and engaging with a different future for the earth and the humans that live on it; it is about finding a language so we can talk about and develop shared practice, interventions and ways of working that are in tune with the ecosystems of the earth. Therefore, this book is a tool for therapists, teachers and outdoor educators, social workers, farmers and land owners, ecologists, leaders, and managers who have an interest in creating a healthy world for future generations. Creating an alternative system, while the rest of mainstream culture continues with the slow process of gradually greening unsustainable practice, is not what I advocate. Instead, I believe it is important to find ways of bringing about rapid, positive, and healthy systemic change from within existing human cultural systems.

While ecological and nature awareness is now entering mainstream education and culture, starting with disparate protest groups and activists, the type of change required to realign Western culture with the ecosystems of the earth will need more than tinkering at the edges. Deep systemic changes in existing unhealthy human social systems will require the work of determined individual change agents from within those systems, and this book is an invitation to be involved in that change.

The desire and urgency of creating a sustainable culture no longer needs further debate, and I believe the time for talking is over. I therefore hope this book will inspire people to think and act in ways that can bring about systemic ecological and social change.

How to read this book

I have written this book partly in the form of a biographic narrative linking the development of my thoughts and experiences in a way I hope is clear. The chapters have been structured to allow for the reader to be drawn into a gradual understanding of this work. By doing so I hope it provides the reader with a guide to the field of nature based work and thinking, that is accessible to the general reader. I have also referenced the work in a way that I hope will be useful to professionals who are new to this field, and are interested in further research.

Chapter One describes the deep impact of loosing an indigenous context has had on our current social, psychological, and epistemological perspectives and how recently in our indigenous history we have lost contact with our understanding of nature's systems in favour of a siloed scientific and materialist perspective that currently dominates Western thinking.

Chapters Two, Four, and Six are shorter chapters that focus on the practice of wilderness experience, working in woodlands, and vision fast as a rite of passage. These chapters are based on my personal experience as well as the experience of others in the field, and provide examples of best practice as well as qualitative and quantative evidence where possible. These three chapters also include suggested design criteria for people interested in developing this work as well as references that offer further reading, practice, or research. I have written these three chapters in a slightly different style to the other chapters, and they could be read as a standalone practical guide to three different types of nature based practices.

Chapter Three is probably the most challenging chapter in the book, since it deals with the complex issues of epistemology, of how we interpret the world. This chapter explores how we might find a common language to describe Gregory Bateson's idea of the creatura and Henry Corbin's idea of the imaginal world. This is a way of seeing the world, also described by the visionary educationalist Rudolf Steiner and was previously described by Wolfgang Von Goethe and has its roots in Gnostic philosophy. This epistemology is explored, because it appears to have a strong similarity to accounts of how indigenous cultures' saw the world, and could indicate a way of deeply reconnecting with nature on a psychological level.

Chapter Five is a brief introduction to the use of three nature based developmental wheels or mapping tools that have been used in nature based work and can each be applied in slightly different ways. They are best understood as guides to imaginal qualities, rather than as a fixed consecutive or conceptual framework. Chapter Six offers a guide for how imaginal thinking can open up different ways of seeing nature that can complement and enhance the scientific viewpoint. This might enable the reader the opportunity to begin to read some of the deep and systemic patterning in nature. Finally, Chapter Eight combines aspects from the previous chapters into an ecopsychological framework of human development that could be used in the formulation and thinking about care plans and interventions that encourage healthy human growth and is based on isomorphic patterns in nature. This chapter also offers an ecopsychological framework for professionals who are working with children and adolescents, integrating aspects of developmental neuroscience.

My connection to nature based work

I have been involved with nature based work for more than thirty years, both practically in my work with adolescents, but also in reading and research and trying to make sense of an approach to nature that can appear either overwhelmingly complex or just too mystical to be of any practical use. My personal journey into exploring a new relationship with nature perhaps grew out of my early life experience of adoption that resulted in a distrust of the human world and an attraction to a connection with nature instead. My path of reconnection involved the study of biology, travelling and meeting indigenous people, working as a Steiner teacher, working as a forester, raising a family, experience of vision quest, my own psychotherapy, and training as a systemic psychotherapist.

During this time, through a number of twists of choice and fate I had the good fortune to be involved in innovative projects where I could put some of the ideas I had been researching into practice by working outdoors with troubled adolescents. This included setting up and leading wilderness experience camps, setting up and leading vision fasts with groups of adolescents, and being involved in the growth and development of an independent specialist college providing a therapeutic education curriculum for adolescents with complex needs through a craft and land base curriculum.

My experience of working in the NHS as a family therapist also encouraged me to join up many areas of research in healthy human development that are not usually brought together. For many historic reasons the different professional practices such as: education, psychotherapy, biological sciences and practical out door work such as farming and forestry are siloed disciplines that use language which is self referenced and does not include an explicit holistic understanding of the links between nature and human mental health.

In this book it was my intention to explore how approaching nature and human development in a different way might bring together different disciplines that would create a more integrated and systemic ecological approach to psychotherapy that includes education and deep ecology.

An in-depth reading of Bateson's ideas on mind and nature could provide a rationale for why practical outdoor body based activities are an effective nonverbal therapeutic technique and the value of the theories of systemic psychotherapy to ecotherapy and nature based practices.

It is my opinion that a synergy of Bateson's view of ecology and the practice of systemic psychotherapy could contribute substantially to the emergence of systemic ecopsychotherapy as a beneficial practice in order to address the needs of our time.

Our indigenous heritage

An awakening

One of my earliest and most vivid memories was an experience I had at the age of about seven years old, when I was exploring an old chicken run in my parents' garden that had been abandoned for many years and become over grown with stinging nettles. Amongst the moss and the nettle stalks I found a small, clean, white, skull of a mouse. I picked up the tiny skull in my hand and turned it over to reveal underneath two smooth and shiny domes of bone, like tiny bone balloons that form part of the structure of the inner ear, and are known as the tympanic bulla. I was transfixed by what I saw, not only by the beauty and smoothness of the bone, but because I experienced this beauty as an intense feeling of wellbeing inside myself. I had the experience that the border between nature and my psyche had, surprisingly and spontaneously, melted away. I had become *one* with this delicate mouse skull and it was an experience that began a lifelong interest in bones and a search to rediscover this deep experience of connection with nature again.

This childhood experience led me to the study of biology, and later systemic psychotherapy, in search of a place where mind and nature connect and to rediscover a feeling of deep intersubjectivity with nature.

New brain, old planet: The neocortex and nature

The collective language of modern Western culture is, according to Carl Jung and James Hillman, based almost wholly on *directed thinking* (Cheetham, 2015). This is the type of thinking that we use to find direction and gain control of our environment when things become unpredictable. Hillman and Jung believed that the current alienation of modern humans from the rest of nature has a *chronic locus* in the use of conceptual language as the only way of making sense of the world (Cheetham, 2015).

Yet, the more unconscious parts of our thinking do not use conceptual language, but communicate in forms, images, and stories that signal to us about patterns and relationships that are often too complex to be captured in concepts. The rest of nature – ecosystems, plants, and animals – use this same type of communication, without concepts, which is transmitted in patterns and narratives that carry information about relationships between things (Bateson, 1979; Hoffmeyer, 2009). In this way nature is very similar to the unconscious parts of the brain, or more radically, nature could be seen as the oldest and subtlest but extended part of the human mind. For over 99.97 per cent of our time on earth modern humans have lived in close contact and communication with this subtle mind that we share with the earth. Currently, the part of the brain involved in conceptual thinking, the neocortex, has lost emotional contact with nature and the more instinctual patterns in our own minds because of it dependence on conceptual language. As a result of this separation the directed thinking mind now struggles to control the world; it sees the world only on its own terms. This book is, therefore, about the relationships between the human cerebral neocortex and the rest of the planet.

Gregory Bateson's unfinished business

It has been more than thirty years since Gregory Bateson's call to understand patterns that connect mind and nature (Bateson, 1979). Yet, the search for a logical and linguistic solution to this problem remains elusive. As Bateson himself famously said, "The major problems in the world are the result of the difference between how nature works and the way people think" (Bateson, 2010).

From Rachel Carson's *Silent Spring* in the 1960s, the threat of global over population in the 1970s, nuclear mutually assured destruction (MAD) in the 1980s, to climate change and fracking in the 2000s, it seems clear that something humans are doing is fundamentally out of step with the rest of nature. We have the capacity to construct increasingly complex human artifacts, but the systemic intelligence that maintains the ecosystems of the earth still seems beyond many peoples' understanding. Despite an endless treadmill of technological fixes and complex explanatory narratives, we are travelling ever deeper into an unfolding ecological disaster. We have fallen out of the dance with nature.

Gregory Bateson (1979) believed that in the development of the biological sciences and Darwinian theories of evolution that have shaped our contemporary view of nature, something important has been left out. Our sense of unity between mind and nature and the sense of being part of a larger whole has been broken, we have lost a more ancient belief in the wholeness or "parallelism" between nature and the human world that can be found in cultures that were more integrated with their environment. Bateson believed that,

> We have lost Shiva, the dancer of Hinduism whose dance at the trivial level is both creation and destruction but in the whole beauty. We have lost Abraxas, the terrible and beautiful god of day and night in Gnosticism.
>
> (Bateson, 1979, p. 18)

This loss, according to Bateson, is the result of a systemic epistemological error, an error in how we think about things that has lead to alienating humans from the earth.

In his study of anthropological writing, professor of human ecology, Paul Shephard identified some fundamental differences between the modern and indigenous relationship with nature. The indigenous relationship was shaped by continual exposure to nature, both as hunters and the hunted, and was characterized by an embodied participation, through hunting, running, walking, and the creation of tools and imitation of patterns behaviour in the animal and plant world. Indigenous mental processes have been recognized by anthropologists as having a sophistication rarely seen in Western thinking, where the environment was perceived in a non-linear and relational way, with less dependence than modern cultures on objects and a perceived objective reality. Nature was an environment encountered subjectively, where a hunter moved as a participant within it, oriented by action and where animals and plants were seen as elements of a message requiring symbolic interpretation (Shepard, 1998).

These skills seemed to equip our ancestor really well when dealing with the discontinuity and complexity of the natural world and enabled them to maintain fluid and yet stable cultures that remained resilient through cycles of climatic and other ecological change; they were able to maintain a dynamic relationship between the emergent ecological and psychological narratives within nature and culture. This is in stark contrast with the fragility of modern culture where our current accumulated knowledge of psychological processes and our descriptions of the science of ecology and biology have remained closed from each other within separate academic silos.

As I walked out: A journey through time

As many young people have done before me, I set off travelling in my early twenties in search of adventure and perhaps more importantly in search of a sense of belonging to the wider world. I was curious about what other cultures did with their time and how they found a meaningful context for their lives. Growing up in Britain the culture around me seemed a little too rigid and removed from some deeper connection that I had fleetingly experienced in my encounter with the mouse skull. In my youth I had spent years searching for this connection in the fields and woods where I lived. Beyond the new housing estates and supermarket car parks, I found fragments of a lost natural history in the hedgerows and woodlands. Remnants of past farming practice, derelict farm buildings and implements, neglected old woodlands and paths, once part of a way of life now abandoned that had silently slipped away in one generation.

The Dead Sea Bedouin

My travels took me out of Europe to the Middle East in the early 1980s. At first I was just passing through unknown towns on buses and lorries looking out of the window on a changing landscape, but as I slowed down to a walking pace this changed. One night in Syria, in early March, I camped at some hot springs where sulfurous water, the temperature of a hot bath, ran in small rivulets and mixed with the cold water streams that also ran through the dry and rocky wadis. I spent the evening bathing in the hot water, close by Syrian workers were beginning the construction of a luxury spa; even here the land was under threat of change. The next afternoon I hitchhiked along a hot mountain road heading south, to my left in the east the landscape was sparse and arid, a land of mountains and huge dry canyons. To my right the land dropped quickly away to the Dead Sea far below, shrouded in heat haze. Beyond that, was the desert of the rift valley, Israel and the West Bank. My reverie was interrupted by a white Toyota pickup that stopped in front of me. I began climbing into the back for a lift but the driver called me round to the front. The driver and his companion were both dressed in smart traditional Bedouin attire, with white dishdashas down to their ankles and red and white scarves around their faces. The driver told me that he worked in the local bank in town and was going home for the day and asked if I would like to stay the night with his family. I agreed and we drove on for a few more minutes and then he drove off the road and parked the truck on the edge of the ravine overlooking the Dead Sea. He pointed down into the valley where there were a few Bedouin tents far below. "That's my home," he said, pointing to one of the tents and then to a small moving dot next to a camel said, "And that is my father".

I followed him and his companion's sandals down a rough goat track into the valley, arriving at the Bedouin tent to be greeted by his father. He invited us into the tent where he seated himself cross-legged by the smoldering, dusty fire pit. In the ashes was an ancient brass coffee pot with a long spout and he stoked up the fire with a few aromatic twigs to heat up the coffee, he chain-smoked and chatted to his son in Arabic as he did so. Coffee was then served in a single tiny cup that we all shared; he drank first as was the tradition when entertaining guests to show that the coffee was not poisoned. The Bedouin women lived in the same tent, but were screened behind a wall of woven goats' hair, and as the sun went down they came out to receive and tether the goats, that the boys and men had brought in from the surrounding hills. She goats with kids were tethered by one foot to loops in a long hairy rope pegged at both ends and the girls milked them into an old and well used five litre Castrol GTX oil tin. The camp became busy for the evening as jobs were completed before the fading of the light. After a supper of goat's meat and milk we strolled in the warm air and looked out across the valley to the rings of lights that marked the security fences of kibbutzim in Israel.

This event was embedded in a both ancient and current narrative of that land. Apart from the Toyota Land Cruiser, their belongings, tasks, and rituals of that day were unchanged for hundreds and possibly thousands of years. Abraham would have had no problem fitting into this evening and would have felt at home. Life for these Bedouin was modern and yet strongly referenced to timeless coordinates: land, family, and the daily rhythms and seasonality of animals' lives. These Bedouin were connected with at least two thousand years of incommensurable and yet fundamentally unchanged history. The goats and Bedouin have been involved in this ritual for thousands of years, but every day was subtlety different. Having been raised in suburban British culture and despite a good education and a

University degree, I realized I was less prepared for this world of Abraham and his ancestors than the small boys who tended the goats. Here something of the indigenous remained intact in a way that was not romanticized, forced, or fabricated.

Loosening the ties

A few days later I had a meeting with a Syrian policeman who confiscated my passport. After a few hours of maintaining the pose of his professional position, he gave my passport back and invited me to his house for supper and we ate together on the floor with his children. He also served coffee in tiny cups that we shared, but this time it was from a thermos flask with a press down dispenser and not a brass coffee pot. Instead of watching the goats return from the hills we watched an episode of *CHiPs* on the television, a series about the Californian Highway patrol motorcycle police. I am not sure Abraham would have followed the show if he had turned up. The rituals of the policeman's family had shifted from the Bedouin context and the goats were replaced by a TV series from another culture, a powerful new story with only a short window of relevant context. The episode of *CHiPS*, although probably running somewhere in the world, is now a dated 1970s TV show destined to become obsolete after a few short decades.

In a subtle way the lives of the policeman's family had been altered by becoming uncoupled from the emergent, creative, and destructive matrix of nature; Bateson's "terrible and beautiful god of day and night" that must have been experienced by the ancient lineage of Bedouin shepherds. The policeman and his family were now linked instead to stories and contexts generated out of the minds of TV producers. The beginning of an intangible and almost invisible disconnect between nature and every day human life had begun.

The Sudan

Having travelled through Egypt and the Sudan by train and bus, I once again slowed down to walking pace and journeyed on foot, walking out of town into the rural villages of the Sudan. I walked through the spiny Sudanese savannah from village to village, following directions drawn for me on a scrap of paper by a local man. Beyond the reach of metalled roads, where people lived on less than a dollar a day, the culture was rich with a natural and open hospitality that I had never experienced before.

The villages were spaced approximately every ten miles and joined by human footpaths and the only indication that a village was close by, were groups of women returning from the bush with bundles of brushwood kindling balanced on their heads.

The Nuba tribes' people, with whom I stayed, were generally very tall and well built and prided themselves on their strength and fighting skills. The men usually moved about naked, unless they saw a truck when they quickly pulled on their shorts as the government had declared nakedness illegal. I spent a few days staying with a Nuba family and their three small boys. The husband was a large muscular man and I helped him collect wood and weed his maize patch a short walk out of the village. One night before supper the husband and wife, equally large and quite strong, fell into a domestic dispute and after a short argument the fight quickly became a physical wrestling match. Husband and wife slammed into each other wordlessly wrestling, and were quite equally matched. The fight continued and I sat with the boys who waited patiently until it was finished, the only sound being the slap of contact of their parents sweating bodies. After a while they stopped the fight with a short verbal signal, both parents sweating and breathing heavily. I was struck by the non-verbal nature of their fight, few words were ever spoken but their wrestling had enabled them to clear the air and re-engage with the evening tasks.

Wealth in these villages was measured in cattle and almost everything I encountered had a natural and handmade origin. Houses made of earth with thatched roofs, knife and axes forged from lorry springs. The local blacksmith worked under a huge tree in a forge pumped by a small boy using goatskin bellows. Other than some metal tools and the ubiquitous twenty-five litre plastic water containers, the type of tools and possessions they used appeared to have remained unchanged for many generations.

The staple diet in all the villages was maize. This meant that it was eaten at every meal, either as roasted cobs or milled and cooked into dough. Children supplemented this diet with grasshoppers that they caught and roasted. On special occasions such as funerals, one of which I attended, a goat or cow was killed and the meat was shared out. Death and the killing of animals was a part of life, animals were killed by the cutting of the throat and was usually accompanied in Arabic speaking villages by a short blessing of "Bissmillah" (in the name of God). All life in these villages was intensely physical and body based, children would run outside to dance and sing in the rain during thunderstorms and adults would swim quickly in swollen rivers that had the power to wash away the unwary.

After one long day walking alone through the bush I arrived at a new village and entered a clearing where a gigantic baobab tree was lit up by the golden African afternoon sun. My arrival startled a group of children, dressed only in a thick covering of orange ochre clay and they ran as silently and graceful as antelope from the first white person they had ever seen. I couldn't help feeling I was seeing human beings in a way I had never seen before: vibrant, wild, and living in a culture where natural and social ecosystems were intimately connected.

Indigenous origins: San Bushman Rock paintings

In Southern Africa, I remember climbing amongst huge boulders under a hot sun, the surface was granular and reddish in colour and had been flaking off under the intense heat and cold of winter nights for many millennia. These bare granite outcrops known as "Kopjes", are dotted about on the southern African landscape and provide undisturbed shelter for small colourful birds, like paradise flycatchers, as well as shelter for nervous green lizards. These are also a good hiding place for snakes such as the legendary and deadly black mambas and this brings a wariness to every movement on the rocks. When I climbed up to the top, the landscape opened out in front and behind me; as far as I could see this fertile and cultivated flat land was scattered with small villages and cattle kraals made of acacia thorns, and dotted with groups of wandering cattle and goats tended by small boys, and the sound of human voices carried clearly in the warm air.

I reached a flat rock outcrop facing the east and found what I was looking for, ancient rock paintings created by the San people or Bushmen, who once lived there. They were the first indigenous African hunter-gatherers forced off the land, first by Bantu tribes and later by European settlers. But their rock paintings where still there on the rock: antelope, elephants and people, hunters and dancers, lively and agile in red ochre pigment. Although the paintings were thousands of years old and the Bushman long gone, their presence lingers with the paintings, they could have been gone for only a few moments. I stayed a while and looked out over the plains the San Bushman once occupied.

All humans share an indigenous heritage and we vary only by the number of generations that we are now removed from the remembrance, acknowledgment, and context of these roots. For all of us, independent of religion, nationality, culture, or race, our great, great grandfathers and grandmothers lived their lives in continual contact and interaction with nature as hunter-gatherers.

At that time, I made sense of my experiences rationally and scientifically based on my Western education. However, this perspective began to feel less important after years of careful observation of plant and animal forms and growth, combined with a long study of indigenous cultures that operated outside of Cartesian dualism. Gradually, defining the boundaries between mind and matter became less relevant than the subtle relationships between people and nature. In trying to make sense of how our indigenous ancestors lived it seemed I had an image in my mind that I could not reach with Western scientific thought; I had run out of language to describe the felt connection between mind and nature. Western culture seems to have lost this ancient knowledge of how to really experience this connection, and now, for the healing of the planet and ourselves, we need it back.

Two different worldviews

In his book, *The World Until Yesterday*, Jared Diamond (2012) writes about the Western fascination with traditional societies and explores anthropological studies of the differences and similarities between the two different worldviews. His own interest began with his work in Papua New Guinea at the age of twenty-six. Diamond warns against the risk of romanticizing traditional practices, but has come to believe that traditional societies have some superior practical solutions to many of the issues we wrestle with in the *Western, educated, industrial, rich and democratic societies*, a description he shortens to the acronym, WEIRD.

Diamond describes the way traditional indigenous cultures approach health, treatment of the elderly, child rearing, and the use of their leisure time. He also points out that the most contemporary academic studies carried out by psychologists and sociologists, are based on generalizations about human nature that are taken from WEIRD cultures. If we are to make informed social choices about human nature we would be wise to include the experience from the whole range of traditional societies. Human cultures have lived in a wide variety of traditional ways for hundreds of thousands of years and the shift from hunter gathering to farming began only about 10,000 years ago with modern life representing only a tiny fraction of human existence.

Indigenous education

Diamond explains how in hunter-gatherer cultures, children's social development is enriched by being given autonomy to explore their environment and where children were rarely restricted access to all the resources available to the adult world. They were frequently allowed to explore and play with fire and sharp tools in a way that WEIRD cultures would consider dangerous. Play in these traditional cultures, where there were no manufactured toys, was with animals and natural materials and children became skilled at imitating adult activities. Diamond describes how the New Guinea coast dwelling children created toy boats, fishing net and fish spears, while children of the Nuer cattle herders from the Sudan made and played with toy cattle in cattle kraals made out of mud. Yanomamo Indian children from Brazil play with plants and animals from the rain forest and become skilled naturalists as a result (Diamond, 2012). Through this sort of play children gain skills and knowledge of the adult world early in life by comparison to those in WEIRD culture. Diamond also provides examples of how infant boys in the Siriona Indian tribes of Bolivia are being given tiny bows and arrows at aged three months old and begin developing the skills of archery at three years. Consequently, at the age of thirteen these boys are fully skilled hunters, having undergone a ten year skill apprenticeship during latency, prior to their transition into adolescence. In fact, Paul Shepard suggests that toys in WEIRD culture "may be a burden to children in ways we do not yet understand" (Shepard, 1998, p. 160), reinforcing a material worldview, that the world is nonliving, objectified, passive, and subordinate to our needs.

There are other important differences in traditional societies, in comparison to Western cultures, such as *allo parenting* where the responsibility of child rearing is widely shared amongst the adult population (Diamond, 2012). Anthropologists have long recognized the important psychological benefits from this, where children experience broader social influences and learning from a wider range of different adults. In this way, children develop sophisticated social skills as a result, enriching the social culture. Due to the small scale of local populations Diamond suggests that someone growing up in an traditional indigenous culture would be surrounded by a only few hundred people, most of whom would be known members of the tribe, or related by blood or marriage, neighbouring tribes and would be known about through word of mouth and stories. The event of meeting a true stranger would therefore be exceedingly rare and so indigenous children grew up within a strong and usually safe but varied container of adult attachment relationships. Diamond explains how these practices seemed to have worked tolerably well for the last hundred thousand years and although these cultures have radically changed, humans remain behaviourally identical, in terms of their needs, as our hunter-gatherer ancestors.

Getting perspective, the long and the short view

The psychologist, writer, and ecopsychologist Chellis Glendenning (1994) describes growing up in the Unites States and suddenly recognizing in early adult life that our WEIRD relationship with nature was almost completely inadequate for the job of surviving more than just a few decades into the future. She calculates that we have spent 99.97 per cent of human existence as hunter-gatherers in intimate contact with the ecosystem of the natural world and the recent development of Western culture has developed into a pathological and addictive environment for the human psyche. Of the remaining 0.03 per cent of human existence where we were *not* hunter-gatherers, most of this time was spent as simple tribal pastoralists. If the whole history of development of modern humans was represented as the distance of one kilometre, then humans became settled farmers only in the last two metres of that distance. If we think of the last hundred years as truly modern, where our social, education, and health systems have been organized by rational and academic study, this can be represented by a tiny fraction of the kilometre journey, in fact it is only the last 2.5 centimetres.

In the WEIRD world we are now making critical and unchallenged decisions about the future of how we relate to nature and human development from the context of only 0.00025 per cent of human existence. To put this into further context, 0.00025 per cent of a human lifetime is approximately two hours. To make life-changing judgments about someone's life based only on an experience of the most unsettled and rapidly changing two hours, which WEIRD culture represents, seems to be a kind of unchallenged madness. But this is currently how the WEIRD world organizes itself and plans for the future, and we do not need to look far to see that this does not work for the rest of nature.

The call of the tribe

The WEIRD worlds' fascination with traditional cultures has a long lineage. In 1937 the archeologist and explorer Thor Heyerdahl, disillusioned with the state of the modern world, set off with his wife to live on the remote Polynesian island of Fatu Hiva with the intention of returning to nature (Heyerdahl, 1976). The couple identified the island of Fatu Hiva as one of the remotest places from Western culture that they could find and after spending many months training they were initially successful in living outside of a developed culture. Eventually they were forced to abandon their project due to infections and tropical illness, ironically brought to the island inadvertently by Western seafarers. Heyerdahl was perhaps an example of a scientist beginning to see beyond the limitation of WEIRD cultures self-referenced perspective.

George Monbiot in his book, *Feral* (2013) recounted his experience in Kenya of befriending an indigenous Masai at the point when Masai culture was to be forever changed by land enclosures. Spending time with these indigenous people in contact with the land he was struck deeply by the thought that if he had been able to choose a life as a Masai over his Western life he would have chosen the life of the Masai. He recounts how through the history of the colonizing of North America, conscripted European soldiers frequently defected and remained living within Native American culture, if they got the opportunity and preferred the indigenous life to their own, despite the threat of death and torture should they be subsequently recaptured. This was also true for Westernized and adopted Native Americans, they always preferred to return to their own culture if they could and considered it a way of life superior to Western culture.

Some years ago I heard a medicine man of Native American origin talk about his traditional sweat lodge ceremony and he explained that it had become mixed with symbolism from the traditional English sweat lodge. He explained how some of the English conscripted soldiers defending the forts, that marked the outposts of the American colonies, were deported as pagan heretics. These were the carriers of European indigenous natured-based practices, who were prevented from practicing in Britain by the Church, and the result of land enclosures in the sixteenth century. They saw an opportunity to live a better life on the other side of the stockade and escaped over the wall to become assimilated within first nations cultures, and became known to the French as "Ceux que couraient les bois" or "those that ran into the woods".

Indigenous values also seem to influence modern culture in more subtle ways. Pinnock and Douglas-Hamilton, in their book, *Gangs Rituals and Rites of Passage* (1997), studied young street gang members, within the youth justice system in South Africa. He compared their self-generated gang rituals with the processes observed in traditional indigenous rites of passage found all over the world as described by Arnold Van Gennep (1961). The street gangs had recreated, without any knowledge of their origins, the three stages of traditional rites of passage that Van Gennep had described: *Severance*, *Liminality*, and *Incorporation*. These gangs enacted the separation from their former lives as children by joining the gang culture and living in a stage of liminality, outcast from society, but not fully initiated gang members. Their rite of passage often involved a ritualized performance of risk-taking such as killing a member of a rival gang. This event was then marked permanently through scarification or tattooing, allowing full incorporation into the gang. This emergent gang ritual allowed acceptance and a sense of belonging into a tribe of urban criminality and destructive behaviour that appears forcefully driven by the emergence of a distorted implicit indigenous narrative.

Growing indigenous roots in WEIRD culture

Western culture is largely embedded in the modernism of Newtonian thinking an idea that society and knowledge form a progression from a less advanced to a more advanced state. This is a recognizable characteristic of WEIRD cultural thinking and based on the conviction that the world is made up of universal truths waiting to be discovered, that problems can be solved by gathering more information. This idea was challenged by Gregory Bateson (1979) who believed that while modernist linear, cause and effect thinking, was adequate for understanding engineering and building machines, linear causality was not adequate for understanding living systems such as natural ecosystems and human relationships. Inspired by pre-Christian Gnosticism philosophy, Bateson explored the idea that objective reality was in fact more complex that humans were able to think about, but could only be experienced subjectively, as an invisible matrix of complex patterns and relationships, that could not be described accurately by using human language.

This physical uncertainty of the world was also recognized within the field of quantum physics and the discovery that at the sub atomic level, objective reality was not a fixed truth but was dependent on how it was observed (Zohar, 1990, p. 26). These ideas both challenge the notion of a universe waiting to be discovered by clever human thinking and indicate instead we live in a *multiverse* of which we are only partly aware, unless we can alter the stories we tell ourselves about what we are seeing. Systemic family therapy grew out of the ideas of Gregory Bateson and works with the hypothesis that all our human behaviour, beliefs, and ideas – both the good and bad – are rooted in a context, a matrix of invisible stories. One of the tasks of a family therapist is to try and help families see this context more clearly and in doing so, empower the family to understand the underlying patterns and systems that maintain unhelpful or destructive behaviours. Like families, cultures are also shaped by invisible stories and some parts of WIERD culture are now beginning to expand our way of seeing, from a narrow perspective that only references the last 0.00025 per cent human history to being able to recognize the impact we are having on nature.

Reclaiming indigenous mental health

We can never fully know what was in the minds of our indigenous ancestors during the last 25,000 years when they, or rather "we", lived as hunter-gatherers in close contact with the natural world. But it seems likely that living within a hunter-gatherer group would have been a context that positively enhanced human mental health and wellbeing. Studies of ethnographic reports from different hunter-gatherer groups indicate that egalitarianism; altruism, generosity, and group cooperation were always highly valued (Music, 2014). This was a time of a relatively stable human population and it was clear from these studies that altruistic groups out competed groups of self-interested individuals. These prosocial behaviours are likely to have helped to develop our social brains and the associated interpersonal skills such as understanding the minds and intentions of others, empathy, and synchronization that maintained tightknit altruistic communities, where children were responded to rapidly and had constant human companionship. Child and adolescent psychotherapist, Graham Music suggests that in this long evolutionary context infants were born into benign environments and this in turn would trigger the release of the hormone oxytocin, the "love hormone" that is responsible for the bonding process between mother and babies and between couples. Oxytocin also reduces the fear response and slows the activity of the amygdala, the trigger for stress, further inducing a sense of tranquilly, empathy, and altruism.

There is a growing body of research that indicates that living in close contact with nature would have further enhanced mental wellbeing. Studies on the effect of experiencing the natural environment have shown that observing or walking in nature has a similar effect as living within a prosocial environment. While nature has the effect of calming the mind and relaxing the unconscious or autonomic nervous system, it also significantly increases the relaxation and recovery time after stressful situations and restoring optimum functioning of the brain (Bird, 2007).

The normalization of disconnection from the body

In contract to the positive mental health benefit of being in contact with nature and living in small hunter-gathering groups, WEIRD culture is now beginning to be recognized as a potentially unhealthy and stressful environment. Current neuroscience informed psychotherapy, exemplified by the work of Peter Levine and Ann Frederick (2012) and Bessel van der Kolk (2014), suggest that body based developmental trauma is the public health challenge of our time, which is characterized by "pervasive biological and emotional dysregulation, failed and disrupted attachment, problems staying focused and on track, and a hugely deficient sense of coherent personal identity and competence" (Van der Kolk, 2014, p. 166).

Being surrounded by environmental and social stress triggers, and the constant activation of the emotional brain (the combined limbic and reptilian brain) results in states of constant flight or fight, and the loss of the ability to self-regulate emotions. Levine and Kolk suggest these symptoms often remain undiagnosed and are usually beyond the help of conventional talking therapy, but can be helped by enabling the patient to reconnect with their bodies through therapeutic mindful bodywork; the kind of activities that hunter-gatherers would have engaged in every day. In his study of the brain, psychiatrist Ian McGilchrist characterizes how the two hemispheres of the brain process the world in different ways, which results in two completely different worldviews. He explains that the left-brain has a tendency to process knowledge from an abstract perspective and within a closed system and to focus on purpose using the kind of linear thinking and language that underpins much of Western thought. Whereas the right hemisphere of the brain, that develops earlier in childhood than the left, sees the world in a completely different way, as alive with implicit interconnections that are always changing and evolving, ". . .and to this world it exists in a relationship of care" (McGilchrist, 2009, p. 174).

It seems very likely that while our hunter-gatherer ancestors engaged for millennia in experiential learning and body based daily activity, they would have little need for the intellectualization or abstraction of the left-brain, the tendency to name, objectify, and categorize that dominates WEIRD culture. Indigenous people were more likely to be deeply embedded in the processes of the right brain, a type of perception that would be open to non-verbal clues and emergent messages from the natural world that has been observed in hunger gatherer cultures.

The normalization of disconnection from the land

Close to where I live in Britain is a place called "the slaughters" where it is said the Romans defeated the last Celtic tribes, about 2,000 years ago. The breaking of the tribes and the separation of people from their ancestral connection with the land has been repeated all over the world and continues to this day as the last tribal groups in the Amazon rainforest come into contact loggers and mining companies. Charities and pressure groups that support the land rites of first nations people, work hard to protect indigenous land from commercial exploitation and illegal land grabs. In Britain this process continued with the enclosures act of 1773 that allowed the enclosure of land as private property. Land that was previously considered common land, where anyone could graze animals and gather firewood, was transformed into a commodity.

In Scotland this process was known as the "Clearances" and resulted in the removal of small farmers from land they considered traditionally theirs, by landowners who sold it from under their feet. The displaced native Scots were shipped to the colonies of Canada and America, where they lived on new land also taken from other indigenous peoples. Further removal from the land continued with the Industrial Revolution when more people moved from farms to urban areas. Urbanization fueled the expansion of human wealth through industrialization of labour and mechanization of manufacturing that was once done by hand. This process is now being repeated all over the world where workers from rural areas move to the towns and cities and accept low wages to make expensive commodities. A short term and unsustainable driver of the world economy as underdeveloped nations industrialize. Land, once common and considered to be sacred becomes real estate and the people who previously lived there forcibly removed.

Throughout this process of displacement, indigenous people have struggled to maintain a connection to the land and traditions in the face of the destruction of ancestral graves and sacred sites, and where tribal identity is broken and forgotten. It seems likely that displaced people have carried this loss as traumatic stories and eventually a grief so deep they are no longer aware they have it (Shepard, 1982).

Then it simply becomes normalized. Perhaps this was what drove the destructive power of colonialism when displaced Europeans, travelling in search of new land, displaced tribal people they encountered, and as the victims they then become the perpetrators.

WEIRD perception of indigenous cultures is often complex and conflicted and touches deep feelings of loss that can become polarized into romantic idealization or imperialist jealousy and genocidal hatred. Bill Plotkin describes how Spanish explorers, discovering an indigenous tribe living in relative harmony with their ecosystem in Colorado, named the river that runs through the region "the river of Souls lost in purgatory" referencing their own European Christian narrative (Plotkin, 2003, p. 248).

Psychologist and family therapist, Pat Crittenden, describes in her book on attachment and parenting, how victims of childhood abuse, who do not receive therapeutic support, have a propensity to become perpetrators of abusive behaviour themselves, unconsciously passing the trauma they experienced on to the next generation (Crittenden, 2008). It is therefore possible that a similar process has occurred for people who become deeply disconnected with the land over many generations.

Studies of self-harming behaviour such as addiction and alcoholism seen in displaced indigenous cultures and now endemic in WEIRD cultures points to links to cultural dislocation, and to addiction as a substitute for psychosocial integration and belonging (Alexander, 2001). Is WEIRD culture now the unconscious perpetrator of the environmental and social destruction once experienced by our indigenous ancestors?

But there is hope. Like many of us who grew up in the 1960s and 1970s, I did not expect to see the world to be as it is today, fuelled by science fiction many of us imagined that the post millennial years would be dominated by advanced technology, where our connection with the natural world would be completely lost in a world of skyscrapers, where food would be reduced to pills, and where nature, death, and decay would be swept away from human life in the wake of modernist scientific progress. In fact, we now see a once unimaginable, global interest and concern for the environment, with international efforts to combat climate change. Recycling has grown from a hippy dream to a global industry. And a new generation of young people have emerged, who are deeply interested in a connection to nature, and inexplicably drawn to our indigenous roots and our ancient connection with the land. Although it is impossible to return to the pre-industrial world that humans inhabited during the Pleistocene, human ecologist Paul Shepard lists some aspects of a Pleistocene paradigm that might still be accessible as part of a healthy and healing practise. Among other things he lists the following:

- Access to the wild, wilderness and solitude
- Attunement to daily and seasonal cycles
- Extensive foot travel
- Participatory rather that audience focused music

- Decentralized power, small fire circle groups
- The centrality of narrative recall and story
- Attention to listening, to the sound environment as voice

(Shepard, 1998, p. 171)

By beginning to recognize how unusual our WEIRD culture is, compared to our long indigenous history during the Pleistocene, can help us to think about the social and ecological damage of our current disconnection. WEIRD culture has become separated from the ecosystems of the earth within little more than one generation, and we now live in an almost completely constructed world. This world of human social constructions and technology is deeply embedded in beliefs and narratives that are self-referenced from a tiny fraction of human history. They barely make sense to the present generation and no sense at all in the ecological history of the planet.

It seems highly likely that the alienation of humans from an indigenous hunter-gatherer lifestyle, which was practiced by our ancestors for 35,000 generations, has resulted in a toxic legacy that we are still struggling to understand (Shepard, 1982). And it is entirely possible that the breakdown of the relationship between humans and the rest of nature is continuing to influence individual and cultural perception; in the same way unresolved early trauma and alienation continues to influence adult perception.

The result of this loss is both psychologically and ecologically destructive and can be addressed separately by biological and psychological sciences. However, a synthesis of these two perspectives into an ecopsychological practice is not yet clearly defined. Despite alienation from nature and urbanization of populations, humans are still drawn to and emotionally moved by the esthetics of the natural world.

Using a long term and indigenous perspective to think about education, therapy, and social care can help gain perspective on social policy and provide a different benchmark for what might be considered best practice. Although we can never return to a hunter-gatherer existence, it is possible to rethink our human development needs from a much wider ecological and systemic perspective. If humans are essentially still physiologically and psychologically attuned to a Pleistocene lifestyle, then it makes perfect sense to incorporate some aspects of indigenous experience that are proven to be effective and developmentally appropriate into WEIRD education and therapy practice.

Chapter 2

Wilderness experience

If the human connection with nature is as important as it seems, then perhaps it is possible for those of us living in WEIRD cultures to re-establish this connection and live in the wilderness for an extended length of time and encounter nature as our ancestors once did. However, despite Paul Shepard's invitation to *'come home to the Pleistocene'* (1998), connecting deeply to nature outside of WEIRD culture is not that easy. Despite increasing popularity of spending time outdoors, camping in nature, backpacking in wilderness, and long distance walking, it can be difficult to really step out of WEIRD culture. There is now a growing appreciation and evidence of the value of extended time in nature as wilderness therapy or wilderness experience and other ecotherapeutic interventions that involve periods of close contact with wild nature (Hine, Pretty, & Barton, 2009).

My own engagement with wilderness experience started after hearing a Steiner schoolteacher from Sweden describe taking a whole class of teenagers on an extended wild camping and walking trip to Sarek National park in Northern Sweden. The teenagers were well prepared and equipped and set out with the intention of walking across a wilderness area for two weeks, carrying all that they needed for this journey. He explained that the parents noticed how much their children had changed as a result of this journey. They told him that their children seemed more grounded and more centred, somehow more mature. As these trips developed the teacher realized that the group needed less guidance and teaching and something spontaneously healthy happened to the teenagers who were exposed to an extended experience of nature by simply walking, eating, sleeping and living in nature, as Paul Shepard (1998) had suggested.

Based on this account I set up a wilderness experience journey in the UK and started taking a whole class of teenagers out for ten-day wilderness experiences on a yearly basis (Duncan, 1993). I prepared the class carefully over the academic year for a threshold experience, starting with a day walk in the hills, followed by a weekend camp in the mountains. The wilderness trip involved ten days and nights of wild camping and walking in the wilderness of Scotland and we immersed ourselves in the other-than-human world. We took all we needed in the way of food, drank water from the streams, told stories in the evening, and listened to the roaring of the rivers at night from inside our tents. After three days the group would invariably relax and the pace of the usual restless teenage energy would slow down, resolving in the now well documented "wilderness effect", the observation that it takes only three days of immersion in wilderness to loosen our connection with human culture, and begin to connect with nature. This has been shown to have a significant effect in relaxing the mind and improving mental functioning (Atchley, Atchley, & Strayer, 2012; Greenway, 1995).

After ten days the group became so relaxed and content they often commented that they did not want to "go back". Years after the first wilderness trip I still meet ex-students who comment on the positive impact those ten days had on their lives. The comments made by the parents and carers of young people with complex learning issues, who returned from more recent trips, echoed those of the class group from Sweden twenty years before. Comments included: "He appears more confident and grown-up. He has dealt with his moods in a more grown-up way and tried to solve problems without ringing his parents" and, "He was 'standing taller' seemed more proud of himself, more adult, and more mature. He was certainly different". Based on these experiences it seems that people change when exposed to wild nature for more than three days and though that change is subtle, it is long lasting and systemic in nature.

Dr. Joanna Bettmann describes wilderness therapy as a programme that addresses behavioural difficulties through a variety of therapeutic and educational approaches in an outdoor environment. The focus of this work is usually on issues of personal growth, therapy, rehabilitation, and education and it differs from other outdoor activities such as extreme sports challenges and boot camps. The daily tasks during these kinds of wilderness experiences involve simple living skills such as pack building, hiking, making and breaking camp, cooking food, and living closely with a small consistent group of staff (Bettmann, Demong, & Jasperson, 2008).

The outdoor context of wilderness therapy is important and provides twenty-four-hour care in an outdoor setting where young people are able to have space away from family, friends, and technology. Most wilderness programmes in the United States last for a period of three to eight weeks on average. Due to the intensity of the experience of working with adolescents with complex issues in a wilderness setting, staff ideally need to have dual training, both in outdoor skills and leadership, as well as training in working with mental health. Programmes such as these ensure clients are safe and provide individualized treatment plans that include individual, group, and family therapy, as well as after care programmes, assessment, and evaluation.

In contrast to programmes that use a purely behaviourist approach, Bettmann's research on attachment and wilderness therapy indicate the importance of understanding attachment and attachment focus therapy when working with adolescents with complex or disrupted attachment history in a wilderness setting. Bettmann's work with adopted adolescents indicates that in wilderness therapy young people have to deal with the constant experiences of loss, separation, and reunion. Where this occurs in nature, within a secure social setting it can become a way of helping young people recognize and understand their underlying attachment styles that are often at the root of their challenging behaviour. However if the staff are able to create a safe enough social container this new environment can allow young people to self-reflect and re-evaluate previously held beliefs. This can have a very beneficial effect if staff are skilled in working with attachment difficulties and especially where young people's families are involved in the process before and after treatment (Bettmann, Demong, & Jasperson, 2008).

While studies have shown that wilderness therapy has resulted in significant improvement between pre and post treatment assessment as recorded by both clients and their parents, further research shows that wilderness therapy is also effective in reducing a wide range of symptoms, including substance misuse, low mood, interpersonal distress, social and behavioural problems, and suicidal ideation (Bettmann, Russell, & Parry, 2012). These results, says Bettmann, were shown to be consistent for up to one year after the end of the programme. In a two year follow up, eighty per cent of parents and ninety-five per cent of adolescents considered the programme effective and were experiencing improved family relationship and participants had maintained school attendance. This research also revealed that results were independent of the young people's readiness to change, since many of them were directed by their parent to attend treatment and did so involuntarily (Bettmann, Russell, & Parry, 2012).

A study of a five-week wilderness therapy programme in Utah, taken over a three-year period, found that adolescent clients had made statistically significant changes during their treatment programme (Hoag, Combs, Roberts, & Logan, 2016). Participants reported significant clinical changes in: hope, life effectiveness, and treatment expectation. The study indicated that there is growing evidence that wilderness therapy is therefore an effective clinical treatment for adolescents (Hoag, Combs, Roberts, & Logan, 2016). Moreover, a meta-analysis of the outcomes of thirty-six privately funded wilderness therapy programmes in the USA representing 2,399 participants, found significant beneficial outcomes in: self-esteem, locus of control, behavioural changes, personal effectiveness, interpersonal skills, and clinical symptoms. The study concluded that for adolescents requiring out of home care and treatment, such as foster care or psychiatric inpatient admission, wilderness therapy should also be considered as an effective treatment programme for appropriate adolescent clients (Bettmann, Gillis, Speelman, Parry, & Case, 2016).

Wilderness experience in the United Kingdom

In 2004 it was estimated that 32,000 young adult offenders were sentenced to prison in the UK. However, this intervention had little impact on reducing reoffending rate, which was measured at over eighty per cent for fifteen to eighteen year olds (NOMS, 2006). In response to these figures the UK charity, The Wilderness Foundation, developed an intervention in 2007 for young people, using a multi-disciplinary approach. This was aimed at supporting a cohort of young people considered to be "youth at risk", between the ages of fifteen and twenty-four years, who had experienced social deprivation that tended to leave them with poor social and emotional regulation skills, and low self-esteem, that often led to further social isolation and destructive life style choices (Peacock, Hines, & Pretty, 2008).

The Wilderness Foundation designed a nine-month intensive course to help this group of vulnerable young people and Essex Social Services, UK, supported the programme (Peacock, Hines, & Pretty, 2008). The profile of the typical participants included: a history of drug and alcohol abuse; issues with anger and violence; poor communication skills; the break down of relationships with school, parents, and other authority figures; and failure of previous treatment plans such as community programmes and outpatient treatment options. In the second month of the project the group engaged in a nine-day immersive wilderness experience on the island of Mull in Scotland, based on the successful model of wilderness experience programmes in South Africa. The South African wilderness walking trails had been used as an alternative to custody and these programmes resulted in the rate of reoffending being as low as fifteen per cent (Peacock, Hines, & Pretty, 2008).

This programme, called The TurnAround Project, was designed in collaboration with the University of Essex, who carried out an evaluation of the programme as part of an ongoing research study. The TurnAround Project included a therapeutic wilderness experience and involved camping and backpacking in nature, as well as involvement in shared tasks like: cooking, setting up tents, and basic living, with the aim to improve personal, interpersonal, and staff–youth relationships. Trained mountain guides and wilderness therapists, as well as volunteer coaches who became the young person's mentors over the following months, accompanied the young people and shared in the activities.

During the wilderness experience the group was isolated from outside social pressures and also experienced the challenge of going through a detox from drugs, alcohol, and technology dependency. The impact of these wilderness experiences were independently monitored by Essex University, who evaluated key outcomes, on self-esteem, mood profile, general wellbeing, and connectedness to nature. The results showed that the self-esteem of these young people was significantly improved after the nine-day experience. Also, there was a slight improvement in their overall mood and participants reported that they felt a stronger awareness of and appreciation for nature after the trip (Peacock, Hines, & Pretty, 2008).

An overview of literature on the effectiveness of 370 different wilderness experience programmes, carried out in 2009 for the Wilderness Foundation, showed that these programmes had contributed significantly to successful changes in participants' health, behaviour, and attitudes. However, the findings also showed that wilderness experiences improved: physical fitness, increased cardiovascular health, reduced fat in body mass, improved sleep patterns, and lowered tension.

Along with enhanced physical health, there were also significant improvements in mental health, self-esteem, self-efficacy, and self-control. These programmes also greatly improved participant's personal sense of belonging, social skills, and interpersonal relationships, not to mention highlighting the long-term social benefits of reduced need for welfare support and involvement with the health and criminal justice services (Hine, Pretty, & Barton, 2009).

Therapeutic wilderness experience involves a combination of a number of interventions each with a potentially positive effect on adolescent psychological health and development. These include an element of detoxification from social media, technology, and the negative influence of their peers; replacing these experiences with time in nature has significant effect on lowering stress. The walking and camping aspects of any wilderness experience has the effect of increasing gross motor activity in a way that is directed and purposeful. Being in nature is therefore not only physiologically and psychologically relaxing, it can provide a safe neutral space for young people to engage with adult carers and therapists and teachers in a uniquely beneficial context. The *wilderness effect* of a three-day immersion has the effect of creating a reflexive space, allowing the possibility of valuable conversations that have previously proven to be too difficult.

It's clear that further development of this work in urbanized countries is a challenge because of the limited access to wilderness areas, not to mention the institutionalized aversion to these activities being perceived as high-risk. Even though adolescents are consistently drawn into risk-taking behaviour, whether it is socially sanctioned or illegal, prolonged experiences in nature has shown to be an effective and economic therapeutic intervention for some cohorts of adolescents. With a thorough understanding of the theory, practice, current evidence, and effective design criteria of wilderness work, it is possible to create safe and powerful interventions for adolescents in a variety of different natural environments.

Participants' voices

Wilderness experience in Scotland, June 2003
Whole class school group, ten days

Participants' feedback

I was sixteen years old when I undertook the wilderness experience. It was a point in my life when I wanted to be given real responsibility and the chance to prove that I was ready to take responsibility.

At sixteen there is a reluctance in society to view young adolescents as competent and responsible and this was a constant frustration for me. The wilderness trip gave me a chance to take control of ten days of my life, a *chance to prove that I was capable of careful planning, logical thinking, physically able, and socially aware.*

I enjoyed every second of the experience, the adventure and the challenges. For me every problem became an opportunity to problem solve with immediate rewards. Difficult terrain was a chance to test the limits of my physical abilities, and wet cold weather was a test to how well I had prepared.

I also benefited from the social aspect. For the first time the group had to work together, to put aside previous differences and look out for each other. While learning about my strengths and weaknesses I also learnt to respect the strengths and weaknesses of my classmates, which I have found useful in maintaining lasting friendships.

The wilderness experience above all else demonstrated how valuable and important it was for me to spend time in nature, and how this environment could provide an opportunity to use and develop key skills. It also helped me to gain confidence in my abilities and provided a wealth of experiences to draw on when making future life decisions. For example, my decision to take a gap year exploring the wildernesses of South America, to study Environmental Sciences at University and to cycle to Hong Kong for charity have all been shaped to some extent by the experiences I had during the wilderness trip.

Thank you!

~~~

At the age of sixteen, a small group of us travelled to North West Scotland. The anticipation was high, as for many it was the first significant time spent away from the protection, or over protection of their parents.

After a grueling eight hours on various trains, taxis, and boats, we landed on the southern tip [of a peninsular], carrying with us everything we would require for the next ten days. The excitement rose, as we realized, should we require anything that hadn't been brought along, we would have to go without.

Being self-sufficient in this way led us to feel empowered and delivered an overwhelming sense of independence. We split into two groups of five people, each circumnavigating the mountain range in a different direction. Our group took to the coast staying low, and covering large distances, while the other group headed inland and climbed higher.

Encounters with otters and rainbow trout were some of nature's highlights, while battling an endless wall of midges and mosquitos at dusk was a particularly testing time.

One afternoon we were encouraged to spend some time alone. The particular place was left to our own choice. I chose a remote part of the river someway upstream where a gently sloping rock lead down into the water. Three hours passed in a flash of daydreaming and meditation, with not another soul for miles around. Welcomed back to camp that night, I believed I experienced something quite unique. Absolute solitude. This expedition was remarkable and unlike any other.

I have fond memories of the bonds formed, the characters sculpted and the lessons learned from this short, challenging, yet incredibly rewarding experience. This adventure instilled in me a desire to explore, a desire to be independent, and a desire to constantly look around each corner for the next adventure.

TurnAround Project
Wilderness trail, phase three, 2012
Youth at risk group, feedback

What has this trip taught you about yourself?

- *That I can get on in a team and I can do stuff and that I am not worthless. I certainly found myself and have let myself go.*
- *I feel better about myself and realized that I can do things. I also feel more positive about life and the future.*
- *I can be with others.*
- *That I rely on others to pick me up or tell me things to sort my head out when I'm down. That actually I'm a great person who has done well given my past. I need to look after myself more.*

What has this trip taught you about other people?

- *That they really are no different to what I am. That I can trust others and work with others without getting angry.*
- *I can get on with people who are different from me.*
- *That everyone has their own story. What's on the outside isn't all of who they are, delve deeper into characters.*

(Wood, Braggs, Pretty, & Barton, 2012, p. 27)

Suggested criteria for consideration in designing a wilderness experience programme

- An experiential programme that takes place in wilderness or a remote outdoor setting (Natural England, 2016)
- Staff need to be multi trained in outdoor skills, leadership, and safeguarding, as well as having an understanding of attachment focused adolescent mental health (Bettmann, Demong, & Jasperson, 2008)
- Rigorous risk assessments, safety planning, and evacuation procedures
- While exposure to nature is therapeutic, clients also need direct support from mental health professionals, including individual care plans, treatment, and aftercare (Bettmann, Gillis, Speelman, Parry, & Case, 2016)
- The structure of the treatment programme can be a contained or closed group or a continuous flow programme where participant and staff join and leave the programme over an extended period (Russell, Hendee, & Philips-Millar, 1999)
- Wilderness experience programmes should provide time away from familiar environment, human culture, social media, and electronic devices (Bettmann, Demong & Jasperson, 2008)
- The length of wilderness experience programmes can vary from a half day to seventy days with most programmes lasting a week (Hine, Pretty, & Barton, 2009)
- Actives should involve a combination of hard skills such as, backpacking, hill walking, and camping with softer skills such as reflective solo time, counselling, or group therapy (Hine, Pretty, & Barton, 2009)
- Wilderness experience programmes should adopt a *leave no trace* camping policy
- Wilderness experience provides an alternative treatment plan to more traditional residential treatment centres (Bettmann, Gillis, Speelman, Parry, & Case, 2016)

Therapeutic wilderness experience activities

- Backpacking, sea kayaking, and hiking (Hine, Pretty, & Barton, 2009)
- Wild camping, camp cooking, and survival skills (Hine, Pretty, & Barton, 2009)

- Reflective solo time in nature for day or overnight (Hine, Pretty, & Barton, 2009)
- Outdoor group task requiring connection, communication, and expression of needs and response to others (Wood, Braggs, Pretty, & Barton, 2012)
- Use of story, myth, and or narrative (Willis, 2011)
- Symbolic connection activities to raise awareness of nature and the relationship with the natural environment (Wood, Braggs, Pretty, & Barton, 2012)
- Immersion in stories of the social and natural history of the land
- Facilitated group skills work
- Use of intentional ritual and metaphor (Berger, 2006)
- Making time for observing beauty in nature (Burns, 2000)
- Use of nature based mapping tools (Brendtro, Brokenleg, & Van Brockern, 1990; Foster and Little 1998a; Plotkin 2008)
- Engagement in long periods of non-directed soft focused play activities without exposure to technology (Atchley, Atchley, & Strayer, 2012)

Evidence based qualitative data on the effectiveness of wilderness experience
Benefits of wilderness experience from a review of literature 2009

A review of current literature for the Wilderness foundation. Interdisciplinary Centre for Environment and Society, University of Essex. (Hine, Pretty, & Barton, 2009)

Attitude to self:

- Improved physical fitness, cardiovascular health, reduced fat to body mass, and increased muscle mass
- Reduction of anxiety, stress, sleep disturbances, and hypertension
- Improved mental health and wellbeing, increased self-confidence, self-esteem, self-control and self-empowerment, and personal awareness

- Improved coping skills, emotional regulation, expression, and accountability
- Reduced negative behaviours, including drug and alcohol dependency.

Attitude to others

- Development of a sense of belonging
- Development of better communication and problem-solving skills
- Improved and strengthened interpersonal skills
- Development of responsibility, mutual respect, and working with a team
- Increase in awareness of others and group trust.

Socio economic benefits

- Increase self-sufficiency and less dependence on welfare support
- Reduced costs of benefit payments, health care and criminal justice costs, reduced crime levels and drug and alcohol abuse
- Increase social adjustment, reduced recidivism has implications for increased social benefit and community wellbeing.

Evidence based quantitative data on the effectiveness of wilderness experience
Benefits of wilderness experience from The Turn Around Project case study

Programme outline

- A ten-month programme, which used nature as a catalyst for behavioural change
- The programme was designed for youth with an average age of seventeen years who were considered to be at risk due to a combination of offending behaviour, family conflict, low income, substance abuse, hyperactivity, being in care, or leaving care.

Cost comparison of similar interventions

- Placement in a secure training centre: **£160,000** per year
- Placement in a secure children's home: **£120,000** per year
- Placement in a youth offenders institute: **£60,000** per year
- Placement in the TurnAround project: **£7,500** per year.

Comparison of reoffending rate

- Rate of reoffending within one year for young offenders **forty per cent**
- Rate of reoffending within one year for young people who receive custodial sentence **seventy-five per cent** (Peacock, Hines, & Pretty, 2008)
- Reduction in reoffending rates in programmes that include counselling, skills training, and group activities **twenty per cent** (DFE, 2011)

Results showed

- A **thirty-two per cent** mean increase in mindfulness of participants' between selection day and post programme follow up
- A **31.6 per cent** mean improvement in participants' strengths and difficulties scores between selection day and post programme follow up (Wood, Braggs, Pretty, & Barton, 2012).

Chapter 3

Mind and nature revisited

Theodore Roszak popularized the word *ecopsychology* and contributed to defining its basic terms of reference as an:

> emerging synthesis of ecology and psychology, the skillful application of ecological insights to the practice of Psychotherapy and a study of our emotional bond with the earth and the search for an environmentally based standard of mental health.

> (Ecopsychology Online, 1999)

However it is not at all clear where the different and somewhat siloed disciplines of ecology and psychology connect, or what Gregory Bateson's "patterns that connect" might look like in practice within the context of ecopsychology.

Gregory Bateson inspired by the ideas of Johann Wolfgang Von Goethe, spent much of his life's work trying to find a link between the disciplines of psychiatry and biology. He made important contributions to the development of systems thinking and systemic psychotherapy, and despite his deep passionate interest in nature, the biological roots of his thinking are not widely understood. However, having spent many years trying to understand the ideas of the esoteric scientist and educationalist Rudolf Steiner, also inspired by Goethe, it felt like I had something of a head start. But it was when I discovered the work of the philosopher Henry Corbin that a potential new and exciting view on ecopsychology immerged.

It is worthwhile having an overview of the territory that Bateson believed got left out or lost in the development of the WEIRD cultural worldview that gave rise to what he calls the *epistemological error* (Bateson, 1979).

This pattern of something lost, the idea of a better time or better place, is a theme that runs through many cultures both in mythic and religious stories, the idea of a lost paradise or arcadia to which we can no longer return (Shepard, 1982). It is an idea that is both alluring and dangerous, but is also a powerful metaphor to help understand some of Bateson's ideas. There are stories that allude to the idea that there might be another way of experiencing the world of nature and the human mind, a way of approaching ecopsychology that exists outside of the scientific and even cognitive framework and debate, but is still vital and relevant.

A journey to the land of Tír na nÓg

One such story of a mysterious lost land comes from the Irish tradition and is called "The story of Oisin and the land of Tír na nÓg". In this tale the young hunter Oisin is hunting one morning with his father Fionn Mac Cumhail, in the Kerry Mountains in the west of Ireland, when they hear the sound of a horse approaching through the morning mist. They look across the lake and to their amazement they see a beautiful woman riding a white horse towards them over the surface of the lake; the horse travels so lightly as to barely make a splash. As she reaches the shore, the woman introduces herself as Niamh of the golden hair and says that she has followed Oisin's exploits and adventures for many years, from a land beyond the world of men called Tír na nÓg. She has come to ask Oisin if he will marry her, as she has fallen in love with him, and to ask if he will return with her to the west to the land of eternal youth, to live with her in the land of Tír na nÓg, where she is Queen. Oisin does not take long to decide and after saying farewell to his father he jumps up on the horse behind Niamh of the Golden hair and they ride out to the west over the sea to the land of Tír na nÓg, a land where time runs backwards, a land of music and laugher and dreams, where men and woman do not sorrow or grow old. Niamh describes Tír na nÓg as being as big as the ocean and as small as an ant's nest, where the cycles of nature respond to human thoughts, where trees fruit if asked, and it rains only when you wish it and the sun sets if you feel tired, so each person can command their own weather. In Tír na nÓg Oisin feels younger and stronger than ever before, and marries his fairy queen and they live contentedly together. But after a year of marriage, Oisin becomes restless and misses his father and he asks if he can return to Ireland to see him one more time. Despite the warning of the dangers he returns to Ireland, but finds that time has passed much faster there, and where one year has passed in Tír na nÓg, a 1,000 years have passed in the world of men and women. Oisin's father's castle is now a ruin and Oisin and Fionn MacCumhail are remembered only as legends. Oisin makes the fateful error of helping some men lift a heavy stone with his new strength, but as he leans from his horse the girth strap breaks and he falls and in touching the earth connects once more with his mortal age becoming an old man and dies where he falls.

While Gregory Bateson was a critic of the Newtonian, Darwinian, and Cartesian paradigms, he recognized the need to define the boundaries of our relationship between psyche and nature. In fact he believed that we could establish a deeper connection with nature through the use of stories rather than concepts. This story of Oisin in the land of Tír na nÓg is a good example, it gives us an image of two different worlds, a world of cause and effect where people live and die and another land, Tír na nÓg reached by a passage over the sea, or in other stories by a secret door or underground chamber; a land where there is a blurring of the boundary between nature and mind, and the world is no longer objectified but experienced as intersubjective. Bateson believed that "thinking in terms of story must be shared by all mind or minds" and that a non-cognitive process of pattern reading might be a way of understanding the complexity of ecology and psychology, and by this he means, the pattern and images of the story rather than the linear narrative (Bateson, 1979). This contrasts with the more common cognitive approach to understanding complex issues and which can sometimes also be a way of avoiding the emotional messiness and uncertainty of relational intersubjectivity.

Bateson acknowledged that the inspiration for his challenge to the contemporary scientific viewpoint came from his study of the work of Goethe, whose work had his roots in the rich philosophical soil of the early Gnostic natural philosophers. Since systemic family therapy can trace its lineage back via Bateson to the work of Goethe it could, perhaps, be seen as a contemporary manifestation of the practice of this work.

What interested Bateson was Goethe's discovery of a way of seeing nature in patterns or narratives that Goethe believed revealed to him underlying organizing principles in the natural world that were being missed by scientists who merely worked with facts and concepts. Goethe believed he had discovered a way of seeing patterns of aesthetic unity in nature that could not be accurately described in words. Bateson concluded that there are a large parts of the living world, that included nature and the human mind, that are invisible to scientific study because they can not be adequately described in concepts, but require a completely different language, a language that uses no nouns or objects, but only relationship, patterns, and stories.

In trying to understand this way of seeing nature that included the invisible and the non conceptual, Bateson explored a way of looking at the world in two different ways, or through two different lenses, that the Gnostics called creatura and pleroma. This old method of natural science contrasts with the Cartesian idea that the world can be divided into Mind, and its internal mental process, and Matter, which has no inherent mental capacity. The Gnostic division into creatura and pleroma, however, is somewhat subtler. Instead of being either mind or matter, the Gnostics worked with the idea that the world was *both* creatura *and* pleroma. All of nature could therefore be described from both a pleromal and a creatural perspective. This is the key that provides a whole new way of thinking about the relationship between the internal world of the mind and the external world of nature.

Creatura and pleroma

Bateson explains that pleroma describes the physical, non-living world, which is "governed only by forces and impacts" and direct physical causation (Bateson & Bateson, 2005). Pleroma means "fullness" and can be seen as the material substance that physically fills the space, just stuff, that is governed by the laws of causality in the physical universe. This casualty that governs the physical world is reflected in the human mind, as our logical conceptual language and thinking. These concepts can be thought of as the billiard balls of a Newtonian universe that knock together and interact with mathematic predictability. And so, thinking in terms of pleroma, thinking like a machine, enables us to clearly and accurately describe and master the non-living world using conventional logic and scientific language. This skill, taught in schools all over the world, has therefore enabled the development of technology, engineering, and mastery of the physical world.

Creatura, however, is a description of living systems. It is the, "Embryology, biological evolution, ecology, thought, love, hate and human organization" (Bateson & Bateson, 2005, p. 20). Creatura means a creature, a beast, or a living thing that has the ability to act and function independently but appears to be outside of logical constraint. Anyone who has worked with individuals, families, or complex organizations that are controlled by unhealthy unconscious non-verbal behaviour patterns, will recognize how these systems act very much like out-of-control beasts. To describe this manifestation of creatura as simply a system, runs the danger of seeing this as a kind of mechanical defect and missing this quality of moving and evolving creatures that can transform themselves to avoid the light of conscious recognition.

If we think of pleroma, as the billiard balls of Newtonian concepts, creatura therefore inhabits the undefined spaces and relationships between the balls, that are constantly shifting and changing, and by its nature cannot be conceptually defined, but only described in metaphors. In this way, Bateson suggested that the living world is organized by its own "creatural grammar" a language more like poetry rather that prose. He says that although this language is essentially non-verbal, metaphorical, and contextual, "Creatural communication has its own rigour" and learning this language, he suggests, is the key to understanding the links between nature and the human psyche (Bateson & Bateson, 2005. p. 190).

In trying to understand complex organic systems such as nature and the human psyche, purely cognitively, we can quite quickly reach the limits of conceptual or pleromal thinking, as nature operates as a creatural organization that has a complexity that is beyond ordinary human thinking; nature is not only more complex than we think, it is also more complex than we can think. It seems likely that Bateson's concept of creatura is the basis of some of the ideas within systemic family psychotherapy that avoids linear causality and uses non-linear questions to flush out the unseen unhelpful creatural patterns in the relationships between family members.

Systemic psychotherapy

In 1971 a group of Italian psychiatrists and psychotherapists from the city of Milan began to take seriously the implications of Bateson's ideas and challenged the "medical model" of psychiatry. They believed that the medical model based on scientific modernism, viewed psychological problems with the same perspective as physical problems that could be diagnosed and then cured with the appropriate treatment. This type of mechanistic or pleromal approach therefore placed medical professionals in the role of experts with a tendency to create a social construction within medicine that objectified patients, resulting in pathologized symptoms.

The Milan group, as they became known, began to look for a more systemic way of working in their therapy practice and developed techniques that recognized the creatural aspects of mental illness that they did not feel were addressed by the medicalized approach. After practicing these techniques in clinical settings, they published seminal papers encouraging other practitioners to adopt a "non expert" stance and to formulate hypotheses rather than answers to clinical problems (Cecchin, 1987; Selvini-Palazzoli, Boscolo, Cecchin, & Prata, 1980). Rather than searching for facts, they encouraged therapists to let go of fixed ideas and to cultivate an attitude of curiosity and to develop hypotheses on the significance of the emergent patterns with each family system.

While the Milan group avoided purely linear questions about cause and effect, which they believed were characteristic of mechanistic thinking that is associated with pleroma, they also developed the idea of asking relational question. They called these circular questions, which involved asking how different family members perceived key issues, questions about what was really happening *between* family members that might give some indication of the creatural patterns or stories of the family system. This practice was one important contribution to the development of systemic family therapy and marks a change from first order thinking to second order thinking, the transition from Newtonian pleromal thinking to more eco-systemic creatural thinking in the practice of psychotherapy. Perhaps this second order approach can also be helpful in thinking about the practice of ecopsychology. So we can begin to recognize the subtle and complex creatural relationships that influence not only natural ecosystems, but also our human thoughts, feelings, actions, and relationships with nature.

Systemic family therapists came to believe that psychotherapy was trapped in a "tyranny of linguistics" (Becvar & Becvar, 1998) with the medical approach that relied heavily on conceptual language or linear thinking, and so began to lose its therapeutic value by becoming too literal or even frozen into a fundamentalism of certainty. Ideas about the importance of language have been developed by the Australian family therapist Michael White in the practice of narrative therapy, working with story and storytelling in psychotherapy (White & Epston, 1990). In a similar way, the stories we tell ourselves about our relationship with nature determine the boundaries of how we are able to think about nature. Being able to be reflective can help recognize the limits of our language and can also help identify subtle thresholds to new ways of seeing nature. A narrative approach or an approach that uses stories and patterns might therefore free ecopsychology from the reductionism of conceptual language.

A Hermeneutic process

The independent research scientist Henry Bortoft also raised the idea, like Bateson, that WEIRD science may have overlooked something important in Goethe's work. Bortoft acknowledged that Goethe's way of looking at the world is extremely uncomfortable, while we remain in the protective bubble of Cartesian consciousness, which is why it makes it very difficult not to believe that this way of seeing is merely subjective imagination (Bortoft, 1996). Bortoft believed that a way out of this difficulty is through engaging in a *hermeneutic process.* The word *hermeneutic* is derived from the ancient Greek god Hermes, the winged messenger from the gods who is associated with bringing what is not yet known into human understanding. Bortoft helpfully compares Hermeneutics to the familiar process of gaining new insight from reading a book. Meaning and insight while reading does not come from merely speaking the words of the text or from reader's own personal ideas on the text. Insight emerges spontaneously, in a hermeneutic circle *between* the reader's previous ideas and the internal verbalization of the words, as an "*aha*" moment and is often accompanied by a feeling of wellbeing. This experience emerges as a relationship in the space *between* the thinking and the visual sensing of the text (Bortoft, 1996).

The practice of hermeneutics is a way of gaining meaning through seeing a new perspective; a way of exploring the world that is used in some relational psychotherapies and the arts but has fallen outside of the official scientific orthodoxy. It seems that Gnostic natural philosophers such as Alchemists, used this type of hermeneutic process to explore the world of natural phenomena, in order to gain emergent knowledge that was neither truly objective nor subjective. Like psychotherapy, but unlike conventional scientific enquiry, the practice of hermeneutics was seen as an initiatory experience that *transformed the knowing subjective* in a process known as Gnosis, or heart knowing (Cheetham, 2003; Cheetham, 2015). Thus the practice of hermeneutics can be used to interpret the language and patterns in the narratives that emerge within therapy, as well as opening the possibility for therapists to read non-verbal signs such as body posture, that communicate underlying emotion and mood through signals rather than words.

Henry Corbin and the discovery of a lost continent

Bateson's description of working within the rigours of a creatural language is well known for being notoriously difficult to understand (Launer, 2001). However when compared with the ideas of the French philosopher Henry Corbin, whose work has been made much more accessible by Tom Cheetham, Bateson's description of creatura becomes clearer (Cheatham, 2003; Cheatham, 2015). Corbin was born in Paris in 1903, and his mother died six days after his birth, perhaps this early experience was a contributing factor is his search for a preverbal language to which he dedicated much of his life. Corbin was not only a scholar of Western and Islamic philosophy and theology, but he also studied music and languages, and mastered Latin, Greek, Arabic, and Sanskrit. Like Bateson, he was deeply influenced by the Gnostics and the work of Goethe.

In the course of his study Henry Corbin discovered a vast historic body of literature that described a way of encountering the natural world that used images and patterns instead of concepts. This was, he thought, a way of encountering the world that was outside the boundaries of Western natural science that appeared to have become marginalized from the whole of modern Western epistemology from the twelfth century onwards (Cheatham, 2003). In his extensive study of Islamic gnostic writing and philosophy Corbin spoke of a "lost continent" of thinking and language that is almost completely unknown to Western consciousness. This world that Corbin described was known in Arabic as "*Alam al-Mithal*", which Corbin translated into Latin as the "*Mundus Imaginalis*" and then into English as the "Imaginal World". In the same way that Bateson believed that his discovery of the Gnostic creatural language had the power to change the way we engaged with nature, Corbin believed that learning this imaginal language was a transformative passage into a world that had been forgotten. Like Oisin's passage to the land of Tír na nÓg, like the wardrobe in the C. S. Lewis stories, and Alice's looking glass world, the imaginal world is a place that is completely different from the reality described by Western science.

Corbin makes a careful distinction between engaging in imagination or fantasy; something that is made up, and the imaginal process he calls "active imagination", which he describes as the activity of hermeneutic engagement with the imaginal world (Cheetham, 2015). Just like Bateson's creatural world Corbin believes that the imaginal world can look like a fantasy or an unreal product of an unhealthy mind, particularly when it is seen from the perspective of our thinking or sense perceptions. Since the imaginal world cannot be adequately described in concepts or verbal language and cannot be observed or experienced by the senses, it sits outside of the intellectual concepts and evidence based data collection of academic work. The imaginal world therefore lies hidden in plain sight and is accessed through a language that is understood by artists and musicians, but which most scientists have never learnt. This forgotten and impoverished worldview now sits between our conceptual processes and our sensory perceptions, like a landless peasant squashed between two imperialist bullies. Corbin himself explains that:

> Between the sense perceptions and the intuitions and categories of the intellect there remains a void. That which ought to have taken its place between the two, and which in other times and places did occupy this intermediate space, that is to say the Active Imagination, has been left to the poets.
>
> (Cheatham, 2003, p. 69)

Like Bateson's *creatural world* Corbin believes that the *imaginal world* is the home of the psyche or soul, a creative space between subjective and objective experiences. Without this recognition the soul lives in exile from its true home as an outcast in our modern material world of linear causality. This is an idea that Corbin explains is very difficult to digest from a WEIRD point of view, so that,

> The very thing that rational and reasonable scientific philosophy cannot envisage is that Active Imagination ... should have its own noetic and cognitive function, that is to say it give us access to a region of Being which without that function remains closed and forbidden to us.
>
> (Cheatham, 2015, p. 44)

Corbin also believed we have lost an important epistemology, or way of seeing the world, a method of encountering the world that transcends the redundant dichotomy of mind and matter, that separates the world into the subjective and objective. Both Corbin and Bateson identify this third perspective, an older Gnostic perspective that has become forgotten, which Bateson calls *creatura* and Corbin calls the *imaginal*, and it seems likely they are explaining the same phenomena. Both men describe how the creatural/imaginal world is organized in patterns, images, and stories that cannot be adequately captured in conceptual language and requires a process of "*active imagination*" or "*heart knowing*" that changes the knowing subject, a process that has a quality that is very similar to psychotherapy.

The creatural and imaginal in nature

An exploration of nature informed by a combination of Bateson's creatural perspective and Corbin's description of the imaginal world might give us a way of engaging the world that could be used for the development of the clinical practice of ecopsychology. According to Theodore Roszak, the field of ecopsychology carries the potential for the development of an environmentally based standard of mental health, if a synthesis of the outer world of ecology and the inner world of psychology can be achieved (Roszak, 1992). Conventionally, solutions to these issues are approached through the pleromal application of intellectual debate and scientific analysis of observed and measured data to arrive at scientific predictions of the future. Bateson and Corbin point to the option of a different approach, a creatural/imaginal or soul centric approach of active imagination, and engagement in a hermeneutic dialogue. Understating this creatural or imaginal language that the earth is having with itself could be the process of learning to "think as nature thinks" (Bateson, 1979).

Both Corbin and Bateson suggest that through our participation and engagement with nature, we can create the possibility of a co-created and emergent open future, in the similar way that healthy human interpersonal relationships are co-created. In fact, Corbin invites us to try out opening ourselves up to these types of imaginal encounters and to observe what this does for our sense of the world and ourselves. Approaching the future in this way can allow nature to be seen as manifesting as an emergent reality, which is recreated in every moment by how we approach the situation, an experience that we also know from our human relationships. Corbin therefore sees psyche or soul as an active mediator, the organ of ideas that are continually creating new reality. This is a cosmology or worldview that is described by the contemporary Islamic philosopher, Seyyed Hossein Nasr. He says "At every moment the universe is absorbed in the Divine Center and manifested anew in a rhythm of contraction ... and expansion ... which the rhythm of human breathing resembles" (Cheatham, 2003, p. 142).

By working with active imagination and the creatural/imaginal in nature, we can have experiences where the perspective of modernist biology is turned inside out, like Oisin's journey to Tír na nÓg, it is possible to really encounter the *other that human world* and step outside of the Cartesian paradigm (Cheetham, 2003). David Abrams described encountering the world in this way, where, "this breathing landscape is no longer just a passive backdrop against which human history unfolds, but a potentized field of intelligence in which our actions participate" (Abrams, 1996, p. 260).

According to Corbin, engaging with the imaginal in the natural world could open a quality of knowing, or Gnosis, in a way that thinking, that is entirely bound to material causality, does not. The current scientific methodology has a tendency to frame phenomena in relation to current theories and models, and could inadvertently lead to a deadening process of intellectual abstraction and close the door to an emergent and hermeneutic experience of encountering imaginal wisdom. For instance, after years of study and deteriorating health Charles Darwin recognized towards the end of his life the emotional limitations of the purely cognitive. Indeed, he said that

> Poetry of many kinds ... gave me great pleasure ... formerly pictures and music a very great delight. But for many years I cannot endure to read a line of poetry ... I have also lost any taste for pictures or music ... my mind seems to have become a kind of machine for grinding out general laws out of a large collection of facts ...
>
> (Cheetham, 2003, p. 96)

In contrast, Goethe's description of his experience of engaging with nature through a hermeneutic process, where he attempted to understand the hidden language or "signals" from the imaginal world, led him into a deeply heartfelt and emergent relationship with nature and to the idea that nature was patterned with reoccurring archetypes in a language that he could learn to read. Goethe is quoted as saying,

> I cannot tell you how readable the book of nature is becoming for me; my long efforts at deciphering, letter by letter, have helped me; now all of a sudden it is having its effect, and my quiet joy is inexpressible.
>
> (Steiner, 2000, p. 12)

If we think of Bateson's ideas on *pleroma* and *creatura*, and Corbin's description of the *imaginal*, it is possible to see these as two different approaches to understanding nature. Darwin's gathering of data and observation of specimens could be seen as a *pleromal* approach eventually separating him from an empathic engagement with the subject of his study and becoming a "machine for grinding out general laws out of a large collection of facts" (Cheetham, 2003, p. 96). Goethe by contrast appears to be engaged in a deeply personal hermeneutic circle with his material. Describing a deep experience of a heart connection to nature, in which he is changed by his experience; with the Cartesian dualism broken down it's almost as if he has fallen in love (Duncan, 2014).

It seems clear that the work of Corbin has influenced the intellectual foundation of archetypal psychology and his description of the imaginal world influenced the development of Jung's idea of the collective unconscious, as well the work of James Hillman (Cheetham, 2015), and I believe has interesting implications within the practice of ecopsychology.

The creatural and imaginal in ecopsychotherapy

Bateson suggests that the language of *creatura* is not only a helpful way of thinking about the links between mind and nature, but that *creatura* has a strong inherent characteristic and tendency towards wholeness. We see this self-healing process clearly in nature. If an ecosystem is disturbed by human or natural phenomena, pioneer plants species quickly colonize the disturbed ground, followed by successional new plant growth until climax vegetation is re-established. We also see this self-healing characteristic in our bodies, as we recover from illness or injury. What Bateson suggests is that this intrinsic self-healing quality of the creatural, that can manifest in human and ecological self-healing, is a transgressive phenomenon that ruthlessly re-establishes and maintains ecological wholeness. Bateson explains that:

> [The Creatura] ... is both tautological and ecological. I mean that it is a self-healing tautology. Left to itself any large piece of Creatura will settle toward tautology, that is, towards and internal consistency of ideas and process. But every now and then the constancy gets torn; the tautology breaks up like the surface of a pond when a stone is thrown into it. Then tautology slowly but immediately starts to heal. And the healing may be ruthless.
>
> (Bateson, 1979, p. 206)

This description by Bateson provides a strong rationale for the embodied therapeutic encounters between nature and the human mind or psyche that occur in the context of ecotherapy. If *creatura* acts as a holographic healing force, it also raises an interesting question about the importance of scale. We know from ecological studies that ecosystems are holographic; in that a small part of the forest can be representative of the whole ecosystem. But if a forest becomes too small it can no longer maintain the ecological diversity to support large species, unless for example, smaller forests can be linked through wildlife corridors. If creatural self-healing capacity is a function of systemic and relational complexity, this can allow larger disrupted complex ecosystems to heal and grow back together. However, smaller separated fragments of creatura such as isolated animal species populations or humans that cannot maintain relationship, are potentially vulnerable to extinction and mental illness respectively.

This idea could raise questions about the viability and self-healing capacity of contemporary WERID culture. Individuals and cultures isolated from nature's healing creatural tautology can survive but are living in environments where they are only exposed to self-referencing pleroma patterns that are often the product of traumatized human thinking or technology.

Despite the apparent philosophical complexity of understanding the imaginal world, Corbin suggests that working with the imaginal is far from merely intellectual or esoteric and that the emotional impact of experiencing the world in images and patterns is profoundly somatic and kinesthetic (Cheetham, 2015). While it is possible to become dissociated from difficult thoughts and detached from our sensory experience, the patterns of strong emotions are transgressive; they do not recognize boundaries of thought and bodily sensation. Strong emotions can often remain in a precognitive state in the form of patterns and narratives, that eventually become our "internal working models" or "dispositional representations" that drive our behaviours and have the power to subsume and overwhelm both our thoughts and senses (Crittenden, 2008). We can observe this happening in mental health states like depression and psychosis, but also when we fall in love, as well as the process of grieving. The human practice of engaging with the *imaginal* or *creatural* predates psychotherapy, and the visceral nature of powerful imaginal experiences such as grief, or rage, can break open closed down abstracted thinking and certainty. Letting go of the literality of our tightly held concepts and beliefs can be a difficult and heartbreaking process of losing control. Jungian archetypal psychologist Romanyshyn suggests, "grief does have the power to break the mind and its will so thoroughly that miracles break through" (Romanyshyn, 1999, p. 143).

Romanyshyn describes how the process of grief following the death of his wife, led him into emotional states where the boundaries between human and nature dissolved. As a result of this experience Romanyshyn studied the difference between modern methodologies in the study of nature and the psyche, which he compared with the older, now considered outdated, discipline of alchemy where the space between psyche and nature was explored using metaphorical language. He believes that at a deep level that nature and psyche are not two, but one and at this level our connections between nature and the human soul become joined by the imaginal language of alchemy (Romanyshyn, 2007). Helen Macdonald recognized a similar blurring of these boundaries in her book about the loss of her father. She processed her grief through learning to train and hunt with a goshawk, where she begins to merge with the hawk and compares the training of the hawk to the process of psychoanalysis, and how this process of connecting with the hawk helped in her recovery from loss (Macdonald, 2014).

The imaginal and the physical world

Recent developments in neuroscience have identified that early trauma can lead to maladaptive behaviours that are a result of autonomic neural responses, rooted in parts of limbic and reptilian brain, that Bessel Van der Kolk calls the emotional brain. These trauma responses can remain in a state of hypervigilance and therefore flood the mind with old body based emotional memories, which switches off the capacity for rational thought (Van der Kolk, 2014). One of the characteristics that make the emotional brain different from the more recently developed neocortex, is that the emotional brain functions largely without language. Research shows that this subcortical part of the brain responds to patterns, images, and rituals, and is also closely linked to kinesthetic and sensory motor functions and non-cognitive ways of encountering the world (McGilchrist, 2009). Working with *creatural* or *imaginal* narratives could therefore have an important place in the practice of ecopsychology, through using non-verbal communication with these subcortical parts of the brain.

The story of Tír na nÓg shows in metaphor, the value of travelling to the imaginal realm in search of a heart connection, and the necessary and delicate risk needed to return with insight to the land of conceptual language. Using a hermeneutic approach to relationships between and the mind and the body while in nature, could reveal patterns of non-linear intelligence and hidden creatural narratives that often remain hidden during talking psychotherapy (Cheetham, 2015). Ronen Berger, a child psychologist and ecotherapist who works outdoors in Israel, uses a narrative approach, as well as ritual. He also highlights the importance of working with a non-verbal and non-cognitive approach, which is particularly helpful when working with children with learning difficulties (Berger, 2006).

Alchemy and therapy

Robert Romanyshyn spent many years researching processes that engage with active imagination, to try and find a form of *creatural/imaginal* communication that both nature and psyche can understand. Using the metaphorical language of Alchemy and Gnostic psychology, Romanyshyn has developed a process that he calls "alchemical hermeneutics": a structured process that facilitates communication between nature and the psyche in a way that our conceptual mind cannot clearly follow. Romanyshyn has used this method in research and also as a method that can also be used as a type of non-verbal alchemical therapy (Romanyshyn, 2007). The practice of alchemy was not, as commonly believed, concerned with *pleromal* task of turning lead in gold, but with the *creatural* task of the facilitation of a hermeneutic dialogue, between the two parallel processes, of transformation in natural material and the psyche, a very intimate preverbal conversation between nature and soul. Tom Cheetham describes this as "The alchemical process for all its chaos and nearly infinite variety consists of movements of the psyche back and forth across the boundaries of consciousness and over the contours of the emotions" (Cheetham, 2015, p. 63).

The American psychologist James Hillman suggests that mastery of the alchemical language of the material world, which is non-verbal and body based, is a therapy in and of itself and these therapeutic alchemical skills were traditionally, ". . .metallurgy, the dyeing of fibers, embalming the dead, perfumery, and cosmetics, and pharmacy" (Cheetham, 2015, p. 67).

Corbin proposed like the Alchemists that the world of nature and our bodies, needed to be actively inhabited, rather than passively observed, and they valued the practice of learning through visceral body based experiences of the material of the world: minerals, metals, rocks, plants, animals, and the human body. The practice of alchemy was therefore an active imaginal engagement in the practical technology of hands-on work, involving the physical encounter with natural materials. Today we might add further practices, that of: cooking, art, gardening and farming, making music, dance and drama, all of which could be a practiced as therapeutic alchemical hermeneutic disciplines; an approach that is visceral and slow and involves non-verbal engagement deep within the creatural narratives of self and the world. Working with materials through the body facilitates the "thinking through things", in the same way a sculptor *thinks* with materials and a painter *thinks* with paint. Through the process of having a physical engagement with nature it is possible to develop an alchemical view of ecology and also an ecological view of alchemy. From this perspective we can begin to recognize personally that at the imaginal or creatural level the human body and nature are intrinsically connected (Cheetham, 2015). In a similar way, what might be considered merely manual work can actually be seen as a form of therapy that works at a non-languaged level by allowing the "healing tautology" of creatura of both nature and soul to connect and have an imaginal conversation.

Corbin describes this experience of encountering nature in a hermeneutic cycle as both personal and objective, and as such is intersubjective, an experience of the world as coming to meet us in the space of the heart. Through this practice, the Alchemists discovered a presence in nature with which they could communicate, which they personified as Sophia, the great mother, who is also known in esoteric Christianity as the black Madonna (Sardello, 2008).

Henry Corbin therefore invites us to not just simply believe in the imaginal world, but to open to the potential of seeing and engaging with the world in this way. It is an invitation to open to the sensuous, embodied, emergent, and creative imagination, beyond the constraints of logic or category, to open to the possibility of an embodied reflexive thinking; open to the *what if.*

Mastering the language of creatura has the potential to break the WEIRD cultural of habit of seeing mind and nature only through the materialistic lens of pleroma. The world of logical thinking and conceptual language is like the water in which WEIRD culture swims and for this reason it is very difficult to see or imagine the world from a different perspective. The imaginal cannot be described in concepts or words and to approach it in this way is like trying to pick up water in our hands, most of which run through our fingers and is lost.

Beginning to master the strange language of the imaginal and to gain understanding of how to work with it opens up the threshold of a new and unexpected way of perceiving the world. We are very familiar with this idea of strange other worlds in popular fantasy literature and films, but Bateson, Corbin, and Steiner tell us that the imaginal is far from a fantasy; it is a forgotten aspect of reality that we can learn to experience through the process of active imagination. Mastering active imagination involves the process of learning to recognize patterns and subtle organizing principals that are not usually experienced through thinking or sensory experience.

Engaging with the imaginal through active imagination is an alchemical process of heart knowing, and it has the potential of opening up new ways of working with systems of human development and psychotherapy that do not exclude deep ecology and soul work. Working with the imaginal also has potential for working with nature in ways that recognize the non-material systemic organizing principles that underpin the complexity of ecosystems. These patterns tell a different order of story from Darwinian evolution and as such a new way to think about our relationship with the earth. In fact, this process of working directly to understand the imaginal is, I believe, a core practice for understanding the connection between ecology and psychotherapy. The work of Bateson and Corbin therefore provides an innovative way of thinking about the practice of ecopsychology that brings the locus of the work away from the intellectual debate and grounds it firmly in the interpersonal relationships of the heart.

Chapter 4

Into the woods

Forest and woodlands, from the tundra through temperate zones to tropical rain forests, have provided human cultures with shelter, food, and firewood for fuel for many thousands of years. The connection between humans and the forest is not only pragmatic but there is increasing evidence that the simple immersion and prolonged exposure to a forest environment is physiological and psychologically beneficial. In fact, it seems the relationship between these two systems, of people and forest, involves a rich and complex feedback dynamic that works both ways.

Creating a sustainable, therapeutic, educational woodland management plan

In the early 1990s I joined an educational project in the UK developing a provision for adolescents who had been excluded from mainstream education due to challenging behaviour and social difficulties, often associated with mental health issues and developmental trauma. The project acquired ten hectares of ancient semi natural broad leaf woodland that had been unmanaged for several decades, as well as two hectares of adjacent pasture. This area had a recorded history of woodland management dating back to 1200 and the wooded valleys had historically provided wood as a building material, as well as charcoal and firewood. The slopes of the valley had been planted with a mixture of beech and pine trees in the 1800s and the pines had subsequently been felled, leaving the beech trees to fill the canopy. The plan was to develop a therapeutic and education woodland management project that integrated the principles of therapeutic education, productivity, and ecological sustainability. It was essential that the woods provided meaningful daily management activities during the academic year, in a way that was sustainable ecologically, but also as a yearly curriculum. The plan was developed in conjunction with the UK National Forestry Authority and local Wildlife Trust so that the work would be of maximum ecological benefit and productivity of the woods.

The staff team was made up of teachers, artists, and crafts people interested in working outdoors, who had an uncommon combination of skills. Teachers were able to manage the complex behaviour of the young people, but often had no practical outdoor or craft skills, craftsmen and farmers knew how to do the work, but were sometimes lacking the skills in working with challenging adolescents. The skill set required for this work combined practical outdoor skills, teaching skills, and a good understanding of child development and combined these to provide a therapeutically supportive environment.

The students who joined the project, were aged between sixteen and their early twenties, and came with a wide range of complex needs that included: Asperger's syndrome, Attention deficit hyperactivity disorder, Autistic Spectrum Disorder, and histories of complex attachment behaviour and associated learning difficulties. These students attended the programme full time and worked alongside skilled craftsmen and women taking part in activities largely outdoors, or in specialist craft workshops, and were supported by the integrative teaching and learning of cognitive and emotional skills. The woodland management was part of a varied practical full time curriculum of which up to eighty per cent was delivered outside of a classroom setting.

Work began by felling the damaged and diseased old beech trees with hand tools, splitting and stacking the timber in firewood cords to season in the woodland for two years. Smaller branches and stick wood was also stacked and seasoned and made into charcoal. By selecting just a few trees to be felled each year we were able to create an annual cycle of felling and seasoning wood, gradually opening the canopy to allow natural regeneration using a method of woodland management called *continuous cover forestry*.

In the other parts of the woodland the canopy was thinner, as there were fewer mature beech trees, but more of the smaller underwood trees such as hazel and wych elm. These areas where there was plenty of hazel were developed as hazel coppice by cutting the stools to the ground and then allowing them to grow back in the spring to produce a crop of multiple straight stems that could be usefully harvested again after a ten or fifteen year growth cycle. Coppicing is a very old English method of woodland management that creates a cycle of opening up areas of the woodland floor to the light that results in the growth of woodland flowers and herbs and encourages associated insects and birds.

We established ten different areas of coppice in the woodland, one of which we could cut each year to create and ten-year sustainable rotation and the yearly coppice cycle became a highlight in the woodland management calendar. The work had a strong seasonal cycle as most of the woodland work is carried out in the wintertime and we withdrew from the woodlands in the spring to allow new growth and the natural regeneration of the trees to continue without disturbance.

Engagement with woodland management requires an understanding of long time cycles and draws the imagination into a relationship with the future, with two years to season timber and ten years of growth in the coppice cycle. Any young pole stage trees discovered during one coppice season, that had promising growth potential, could be left to grow on and checked again in ten years' time in the next cycle. The old squirrel damaged beech trees, planted by Victorian foresters one hundred years ago were felled, allowing sunlight to trigger the germination of new tree seeds that might in turn take one hundred years to reach maturity. These old methods of woodland management have been carried out in British woodlands for hundreds and perhaps thousands of years, before they became uneconomic. We therefore had the opportunity to join a privileged lineage of foresters and wood-cutters. All of us were silently awed by the dynamic complexity and beauty of the woodlands, which gradually manifested its ancient heritage, slowly changing day-to-day, month-to-month, year-to-year, and decade-to-decade.

Into this subtle, but gentle matrix of relationships stepped the decontextualized and traumatized young people and their tutors and the woodland work became their therapeutic and educational classroom. The staff and students involved in this work were exposed to a powerful externalized ecological narrative, where the changing seasons and growth of the trees, the value of woodland products, and practical skills provided non-negotiable external boundaries. The work was viscerally embedded in the changing seasons; the approaching woodland spring could be read each day, in the gradually changing of bird song and increased nest-ing activities, the opening tree bud, and the emergence of spring flowers in the woodland floor. The whole experience was largely non-verbal and body based. Through the sensory motor learning of the shared work that was embedded in a supportive social and ecological context, we experienced an embodied engage-ment with the imaginal.

There seem to be three main theories as to why encountering nature is a thera-peutic experience. These are: (1) the Biophilia hypothesis; (2) the attention resto-ration theory; and (3) psychophysiological stress recovery theory.

The Biophilia hypothesis

The Biophilia hypothesis that was developed by evolutionary biologist Edward O. Wilson (Wilson, 1984) is based on the idea that we have a genetic tendency to connect with and to love nature, not only because it has been our source of physi-cal sustenance for thousands of years, but also because it satisfies in us our deep need for meaning and attachment. Biophilia is essentially the idea that we are evolutionarily predisposed to feel more content and function more effectively in a natural environment (Bird, 2007).

Learning how to activate this deep experience of connection with nature could be an essential part of a therapeutic education and nature based programme, even though this connection sometimes comes in unexpected ways. Indeed, I once worked with a young man who had been brought up in an urban environment, but had become sensitized to a connection with nature from his experience of repeat-edly handling vegetables while working as a shelf stacker in his local supermarket.

Experiencing nature connection through the body

My training as a Waldorf teacher, based on the ideas of Rudolf Steiner, has influ-enced my thinking about human development. Steiner, who acknowledged the inspiration of Goethe and the Gnostic natural philosophers, described a way of experiencing the world that closely resembles the imaginal, and a hermeneutic practice that is remarkably similar to Corbin and Bateson. This way of thinking is not dependent on sense observations or ideas but an experience of images and connecting patterns. Steiner describes this method as one that required a type of "Conceptual thinking without regard to any definite perceptual content" in order to achieve "sense free thinking" (Steiner, 2000, p. 146).

By combining Bateson and Corbin's descriptions of the imaginal with those of Steiner's can provide new insight for how to work in practice with some of Steiner's more difficult ideas, such as the etheric and astral bodies, two invisible energetic fields that he believed connect nature and the human physiology. These appear to be two different aspect of the imaginal: (1) the Etheric body that is similar to "Chi" and well known to students of Eastern medicine, and popularized as "the force" in the Star Wars films (Star Wars, 1997); and (2) the astral body, which is a more emotionally patterned aspect of the imaginal that we share with the animals.

Waldorf educators make use of the body as a vehicle for deep learning, engaging in our unconscious body senses as a way of supporting healthy developmental embodiment in children; an approach that is now supported by research in neuroscience (Van der Kolk, 2014). Waldorf teachers focus on four particular body senses that are useful developmentally in working with young children and adolescents:

- The sense of touch.
- The sense of balance.
- The kinesthetic sense; the sense of movement in space.
- The somatic sense; a sense of the inside of our body.

I was interested to see how these ideas might work in practice, and if prolonged exposure to nature had a healing effect on adolescents with complex needs.

Touch; the boundary of self and the world

While prolonged exposure to these embodied sensory experiences were common to indigenous cultures, they are now increasingly rare in WEIRD cultures; they have been replaced by increasing screen based entertainment and education systems. Adolescents on the autistic spectrum often have a sensitivity to touch and are reluctant to be touched or touch unfamiliar objects with their hands. It seems possible that creating meaningful contexts to have opportunities to touch different natural materials can encourage a gradual increased awareness of the boundaries between self and the world. This learning can gradually create a transfer from an experience of physical touch, to a more developed awareness of the subtler social boundaries, in a way that can be more effective than purely cognitive social learning.

These types of body senses can be seen as a window into our connection with the physical world. And when the educational experience is experiential, particularly in nature or in practical work based learning, it is possible to work directly with these senses. Experiential learning, or learning through doing, naturally follows the neuro pathways of the brain during childhood maturation and is particularly useful where learning is developmentally delayed. This can be especially effective where students have some difficulties with cognitive learning.

Balance and movement; learning to inhabit the body

However, adolescents who cannot keep still or concentrate in classroom settings, and who are often assessed and diagnosed with ADD or ADHD, can also benefit from practical work and nature based learning experiences. There is evidence that the symptoms of children with ADHD can be reduced by thirty per cent after engaging in outdoor activities, compared to similar actives in an indoor environment. A study of 406 children with ADHD showed a significant increase in the ability to control symptoms after exposure to green spaces (Kuo & Faber, 2004).

In practical settings, where students are engaging in meaningful work in a social context, it is possible to work directly on helping them focus and control their body sense of balance and body awareness, the kinesthetic sense. Young people are less likely to engage if they do not feel the activity is meaningful, or if they think that the experience is too abstract or not real enough. A young man on the autistic spectrum that I worked with used to help his father work on his truck in the yard where he worked as a mechanic, but could not be persuaded to engage in similar activities at school. Thus adolescents often respond positively to supportive adult role models who can teach them work skills they want to learn, but this can only happen where they feel it is safe.

Without adults who are trauma informed and know how to nurture adolescents in a healthy way, work places where young people can potentially learn practical skills can be abusive and re-traumatizing environments. Adolescent boys often find gross motor activities, such as chopping wood, moving heavy object, digging and demolition, are usually most easily accessible. But once a trusting relationship is established it is possible to teach increasingly fine motor skills that are transferable to practical work and paid employment. While the development of fine motor skills and subtle body self-awareness is a helpful prerequisite for cognitive learning, the opposite is not always true. Cognitive learning does not usually lead to a calmer and more focused embodiment in adolescent who show indications of ADHD.

The somatic sense; experiencing the imaginal through the body

Adolescents who have experienced trauma and suffered from prolonged dissociative states often have very little internal body awareness and are unable to describe their feelings, a condition known as alexithymia (Van der Kolk, 2014). Those who suffer with alexithymia therefore do not know how they feel emotionally, and often have a limited capacity to recognize what they feel in their bodies in the way of hunger, thirst, and tiredness, or even sense of temperature. I worked with a young man on the autistic spectrum who had no awareness of his body temperature, and would only wear a t-shirt and track suit bottoms winter and summer, it was only on the top of a mountain in freezing wind that he finally felt cold and asked for gloves and this was his first step to learning how to relate to others.

A young person's awareness of their somatic sense can sometimes be felt in a handshake and the feel of the muscle tone, which can be overly relaxed and limp, or in a constant state of tension. When working with adolescents in these conditions it can be helpful to use the opportunities of practical work and nature based learning to assist the embodiment of a somatic sense, the sense of the inside of the body. We can support these adolescents to develop the feeling awareness of their muscles by experiencing weight, through lifting or moving objects or handling delicate objects, such as baby chicks or egg shells, in a safe social or work context. The experience of muscle tiredness and awareness of their own body strength or weakness can then awaken a useful self-awareness of how they really feel inside themselves through their somatic sense. This knowing of things from the inside increases self-awareness and helps in the process of mentalisation and the recognition that others might also have internal feelings.

Working with the somatic sense can also provide insights to inner mental states. A boy I worked with on the autistic spectrum, who had no awareness of muscle tone and could not use his muscles, was asked to move a heavy load. He would strain and push, all the time while making faces at me, as if he was over exerting himself, but his muscles remained limp and the load never moved. On the other hand, I also worked with a young woman with a complex attachment history, whose locus of control was entirely focus inwardly on her inner muscle tone. In contrast she always brought her whole body muscle tension to engage in practical tasks, but was less focused on social engagement.

Attention restoration theory and undirected attention

Another important theory as to why nature is therapeutic is the attention restoration theory developed by psychologists Stephen and Rachel Kaplan (Bird, 2007). Their theory is based on evidence that being in the natural environment is very effective for restoring attention, and as well as being a restorative experience for the brain because it has the effect of relaxing the prefrontal cortex. This idea makes the important distinction between "*directed attention*" that is required to engage in human culture and education, and activities such as has reading, writing, and screen watching, and soft focus or "*undirected attention*" – the involuntary attention or fascination of relaxing by observing events without needing to control them. While directed attention requires effort and can lead to direct attention fatigue (DAF) with symptoms that are remarkability similar to attention deficient hyperactively disorder (ADHD), *soft focus* requires no effort and is calming and allows for the mind to clear and settle into a more reflective, less directed, and relaxed state. William Bird describes how this relaxing state of soft fascination can be encouraged by moving to a new and interesting environment, which is rich in sensory experiences that can capture attention, but do not require any sort of task or demand and nature, and natural environments can provide such an experience (Bird, 2007). Working with adolescents outdoors in therapeutic nature based activities, and by creating interesting and relaxing natural environments, can evoke this relaxing soft fascination that is restorative, particularly in cases of DAF and ADHD.

Psychophysiological stress recovery theory deep brain relaxation

Psychologist Roger Ulrich developed the psychophysiological stress recovery theory that is based on the activation of a stress-reducing reflex in the limbic system of the brain after exposure to views of nature. Since the limbic system is connected with our autonomic nervous system and implicit, unconscious memory, where preverbal traumatic experiences are "remembered" in the body, they can be calmed by deep brain relaxation and it is this effect that Ulrich believes is brought about by being in nature. We can see this by carefully observing the body language and conversions styles of young people after short or prolonged exposure to nature. This reflex can therefore be used as an effective calming nature based intervention.

Ulrich's theory that exposure to natural environments that include open spaces, non-threatening wildlife, plants, and flowing water, produces an involuntary reaction deep in the brain that quickly reduces the natural human stress response is supported by research. He explains how exposure to nature essentially causes rapid reduction in body based stress indicators, such as heartbeat, reduced adrenaline, and muscle tension, and restores the body to a recovery state after traumatic tension (Ulrich, 1983).

Likewise, studies in Japan have researched the effects of spending short periods of only twenty minutes exposure in a forest environment and found this has a significant calming effect. Forest bathing or "Shinrin-Yoku" was a term coined by the Ministry of Agriculture, Forestry, and Fisheries in Japan and is now used as a beneficial treatment for mental and physical health for government workers. Subjects reported feeling calmer after sitting and walking in a forest environment compared to a city and measurements showed reduced blood flow to the prefrontal cortex of the brain, as well as reduced cortisol levels in their saliva. This study strongly indicates that Shinrin-Yoku activities such as walking and exposure to forest environments, has a beneficial effect on human wellbeing (Park et al., 2007).

Importance of place

In his work with children who have special needs, Ronen Berger from the Nature Therapy Centre in Israel, highlights the therapeutic importance of the "setting" when working in nature. Unlike a clinical setting, nature is not under our control and is constantly changing and often in unpredictable ways that can influence a session. Therefore, Berger suggests that working non-verbally and non-cognitively with his children with learning difficulties allowed for the emergence of a therapeutic restorative body based experience that might not have happened in a clinical setting. In this way nature became an active part of the therapeutic process and the therapist is simply in the role of the facilitator. Berger states that working with a three-way relationship of "client-therapist-nature" can allow the therapist to move between a facilitating role and a witness role, where process and insight occur in the encounter between nature and the client (Berger, 2006).

Experiential learning: processes and culture

Nature based experiential learning that involves the interactions between the client, therapist, and nature is clearly a form of systemic therapy, and this approach can also be transferred to different settings and still retain its therapeutic value, particularly if these activities are consciously embedded in an ecological context and a meaningful social narrative. Young people who have experienced a disruption in their life, through learning difficulty, neglect and abuse, or being in care, are often hungry for a meaningful social context. Practical and nature based work can provide the social scaffolding and an experience of coherence, which is both concrete and also rich in non-verbal metaphors of the complex processes of personal and cultural change. These principles can be transferred to most practical actives such as: farming, horticulture, cooking and food preparation, basket making, leatherwork, metal work, pottery, stained glass work, soap making and paper making. In fact any of the primary crafts and land work skills from the local pre-industrial culture are likely to be equally effective (Duncan, 2013).

Without an understanding of the subtlety of the imaginal world as an organizing agent in ecosystems and human development, it is easy to see why WEIRD culture has adopted the habit of thinking of education as a purely intellectual process. From this perspective, thinking and intellectual understanding is favoured over practical understanding, which has become undervalued as merely manual labour. This makes historic sense in pre-industrial societies where physical activity was an inevitable part of life and children grew up with a strong sense of physical embodiment prior to any type of cognitive learning. Increasing numbers of young people now begin intellectual education in early childhood and have a limited experience of practical engagement in the world. This situation becomes more problematic where young people have experienced developmental trauma through neglect or abuse that prevents them being able to engage with learning in a school environment.

Combining what we know about ancient hunter-gatherer child rearing practice with more recent neurodevelopment research might provide a useful template for healthy child and adolescent development. With this in mind it is possible to create experiences that can recapitulate stages of body based learning that help build positive implicit memories, that can become an essential prerequisite for healthy psychosocial development. This chapter provides some examples of how this type of bottom-up body based experiences can be used to enhance learning.

Participants' voices

Bottom up and body based learning

The following examples were taken from testimonials of students with special educational needs who participated in a broad curriculum of craft and land-based activities at an independent specialist college

- *I am more confident in myself, in what I do and say, and how I act rather than hiding what I am. This confidence will now help me to go on to mainstream college.*
- *I could never imagine I would have changed so much. I cannot find words to describe what this college has done for me.*

Overall findings of a 2010 Ofsted report said: *"Self-confidence increases significantly and students develop social and communication skills and their ability to manage their own behaviour particularly well"* (Duncan, 2013, p. 23).

Coppice work

A case study of research by the UK Charity "Goods from Woods" gathered evidence of students with special educational needs who attended an independent specialist college and were involved coppicing work as part of the woodland management in 2011. The project explored ten different outcomes and recorded the student's comments using video interviews. After the four months' work, results showed that the student were able to feed back that they felt:

- They were seen as more competent by others
- They felt more purposeful

- They experienced more positive emotions and improved mood.
- They also reported feeling that they had developed themselves and felt safer and more supported within the social relationships of the team.

The students were interviewed and their responses recorded a number of different questions as part of the research.

How has this work improved your experience of positive emotions and mood?

- *I like everything, it's really nice and peaceful, it's nice to be outside,*
- *I enjoy processing the wood using a billhook, I didn't think I would like coppicing but I really like it.*

How has this work improved your feeling of being safe and supported within and through social relationships?

- *We get on really well when we do team work like splitting logs.*
- *[I like] Um, splitting and working really hard, enjoy the company and being outside and things like that. It's been quite good fun. Its good.*

How has this work help you to feel relaxed?

- *Yes and I don't know it's like peaceful and the fire's nice and warm.*

How has this work helped you feeling closeness to the natural world?

- *Nice, it's nice and calm, touching the trees, getting into the trees, you felt like a tree, you know. you feel like you're there.*

(Tomlinson, 2011).

Suggested design criteria for therapeutic education woodland activities

A study commissioned by Natural England (Natural England, 2016) identified the three key components of effective nature based interventions as;

1   Meaningful activities
2   Taking place in the natural environment
3   That these activities take place within a social context.

With these in mind some of the essential design criteria in the creation of a therapeutic education woodland programme include the following:

Design criteria

- Recruitment of a staff team that have the unique skill combination of being professionally trained and experienced in practical activities, teaching and working therapeutically and who are respectful and able to work with traumatized adolescents.
- Locating and creating a meaningful outdoor learning and work place environment where actives can take place in a context of production and creativity rather than being explicitly educational or therapeutic.
- Create a culture of "learning by doing" that is role modeled by skilled adults who teach by working alongside young people, rather than by didactic direction or explicit teaching.
- Creating a "learning through work" environment where the "job is the boss" and the where the processes are as far as possible transparent and explicitly linked to knowledge of the social and natural history of the environment.
- Creating opportunities for working for prolonged periods that are experientially linked to the natural seasonal cycles.

Therapeutic educational woodland activities

- Exposure to changing seasonality of the environment
- Exposure to long time cycles, two years for seasoning wood, ten years coppice cycle's 100-year tree growth cycles

- Build fires
- Charcoal making
- Brewing tea and cooking over a fire or brazier
- Controlled destruction by clearing and slashing vegetation
- Felling small and large tress with and tools and power tools
- Stacking and moving timber; splitting, stacking, and delivering firewood
- Learning new practical skills and environmental awareness
- Foraging and eating wild plant foods
- Skinning and butchering animals and cooking meat outside; deer, rabbits, pheasants.

The evidence based qualitative data for therapeutic education woodland activities

Evidence of effectiveness

Research clearly shows that there is an increasing mental burden in the UK, which has resulted in a 165% increase in the prescribing of anti-depressant drug in England between 1998 and 2012. This has increased the medication costs to £1.2 billion per year, spent on drug prescriptions, and £53.6 billion a year as the estimated human cost of mental illness due to reduced quality of life, suffering pain, disability, and distress. Research shows that nature based interventions have the potential in some cases to be a viable alternative to medication. (Natural England, 2016)

The recorded mental health benefits of nature base interventions, that included social and therapeutic horticulture, environmental conservation, and care farming have been shown to include:

- Psychological restoration and increased general mental wellbeing
- Reduction in depression, anxiety, and stress related symptoms
- Improvement in dementia related symptoms
- Improved self-esteem, confidence, and mood
- Increased attentional capacity and cognition
- Improved happiness, satisfaction, and quality of life

- Increased sense of peace, calm, or relaxation
- Increased feeling of safety and security
- Increased social contact, inclusion, and sense of belonging
- Increase in work skills, meaningful activity, and personal achievement.

Chapter 5

Maps and territories

Our current hopes and fears for the world are strongly influenced by our belief in the modernist Western cultural scientific paradigm, beliefs that challenge this view, might be considered to be unscientific, primitive, or unsound. This modernist belief system based on the concrete reality of facts has become the orthodoxy of WEIRD culture, replacing the modernist Christian belief system that is at the root of Western culture. However, the post-modern perspective in psychotherapy has opened the way for the possibility of thinking about the world in different ways that are free from old certainties, and presents the possibility of holding a social constructionist perspective; the idea that we construct our own reality in the process of describing it. From this perspective other emergent world views are accessible; simply by changing the language we use to describe what we see, we can change our perspective or our lens on the world.

According to researchers Timothy Freke and Peter Gandy (1999) contemporary Christianity originated as a socially constructed state religion created by Eusebius of Caesarea for the Emperor Constantine. They discuss how much of the New Testament was based on older Gnostic gospels that were not historical accounts of events, but were allegorical stories, rich is symbols and metaphors, describing the journey of the soul. These Gospels provided guidance and instruction on how to achieve a balance between an immortal emergent spiritual self they call the "*Daimon*" and the body based mortal self called the "*Eidolon*", offering a sort of ancient psychotherapy (Freke & Gandy, 1999).

Feke and Gandy's research also shows that the Christian gospels were based on the Gnostic gospels, but were later transformed into stories of literal historical events. Hence the psycho-spiritual allegories were edited out and suppressed by Eusebius to create the New Testament that we know today. Since Constantine wanted a unified state with one God and one religion to consolidate his idea of one Empire and one emperor, and Eusebius's work proved to be remarkably successful (Freke & Gandy, 1999). Christian religious ideas on human development and on our relationship with nature therefore formed the basis of WEIRD thinking and culture for two millennia.

However, in 1945 Eusebius's legacy began to unravel when a Bedouin shepherd discovered a hidden library of scrolls in the desert at Nag Hammadi, in Israel, known as the Dead Sea scrolls. These scrolls that date back to 390 AD, appeared to be various Gnostic gospels that were excluded from the New Testament. Since then these rediscovered Gnostic ideas have come to influence a number of modern thinkers and can even be identified in aspects of contemporary psychotherapy practice, particularly those with a lineage to Carl Jung and Gregory Bateson (Bateson, 1975; Bateson & Bateson, 2005; Hoeller, 1982). The historic suppression of these worldviews means that very little of these pre-Christian ideas remained in European culture. Although these beliefs can be found pan culturally, and they have been maintained within some indigenous cultures for centuries.

Whereas WEIRD ideas on education and human development are usually based on perceived cultural needs and are altered by changes in government and political direction, indigenous nature based models are informed by imaginal qualities in nature, as a source of metaphor to scaffold thinking about the process of human development. These nature based developmental wheels have been passed down through oral traditions, in some cases for 15,000 years, and represent an older and alternative view that challenges the cultural heritage of European pedagogy.

Working with nature based developmental wheels

The authors of *Reclaiming Youth at Risk*, Larry Brendtro, Martin Brokernleg, and Steve Van Broken, suggest that rather than an out dated traditional belief system, these philosophies of child development could be an important birthright for all the worlds' children, underpinned by a non-Western psychological wisdom that could provide the basis for an effective alternative education and youth development system (Brendtro, Mitchel, & McCall, 2009). The central purpose of education, according to traditional Native American child rearing philosophy, is based primarily on the empowerment of children; ideas that are now supported by research (Brendtro, Mitchel, & McCall, 2009). This evidence shows that the fostering of self-esteem is the primary goal in socializing all children, while lacking a sense of self-worth leaves young people vulnerable to poor psychological and social development, as well as learning problems (Brendtro, Mitchel, & McCall, 2009; Music, 2014).

In contrast to the rigours of most Western thought, these nature based models seem to be quite simple and are characterized by their archetypal or imaginal nature, but have a surprising depth and power in their practical application to teaching and therapy.

The starting point for the nature based developmental maps that are described later, is depicted as a circle that is divided into four quadrants — these can be seen as the four seasons of the northern hemisphere, Spring, Summer, Autumn, and Winter. This image appears in various religions and cultures from across these regions and is often referred to as the Solar Cross, with the cardinal points representing the points of the compass, North, South, East, and West, and also the position of the sun at the Equinoxes and Solstices (Foster & Little, 1998a, p. 35). Although these seasons are not pan global, they can be recognized in the ecology, climate, and cultures of the northern landmasses of Europe, Africa, Asia, and North America. In contrast to the heliocentric astronomical worldview, with the sun in the centre, this is a geocentric Earth based perspective. This is the perspective experienced by humans, animals, and plants, witnessing the phenomena of the changing seasonal pathway of the sun through the passage of the year, from a fixed point on the surface of the earth.

The image of the solar cross can also be identified in the Celtic cross, the cross and the circle, as well as in the alignment of many Neolithic monuments in Britain and Europe, and is an image that predates the later Christian images of the crucifixion. We see this image in the alignment of European churches and the medieval cathedrals, which were often built on former pagan sacred sites that were also oriented to the cardinal points.

The circle of courage, a social and cultural developmental wheel

The Circle of Courage (Figure 1), that is described in the book *Reclaiming Youth at Risk* (Brendtro, Brokenleg, & Van Brockern, 1990), is a developmental wheel based on the Native American Lakota tradition, and illustrates the four basic components of self-esteem. These four qualities create a "medicine wheel" based on the cardinal directions, surrounding a person who stands in the middle of the wheel. The wheel represents four essential developmental stages, and like the turning of the seasons, each has its foundation in the previous stage and once complete moves naturally to the next. This process is non-linear and, like the seasons, the cycle returns and repeats as a developmental spiral through time. These four stages are: Belonging, Mastery, Independence, and Generosity or Attachment, Achievement, Autonomy, and Altruism (Brendtro, Brokenleg, & Van Brockern, 1990).

What makes *Reclaiming Youth at Risk* a somewhat unique book is that the authors have integrated traditional indigenous wisdom with contemporary education and psychology into a practical guidebook. It combines some of the best practice of child rearing from a traditional Lakota perspective, along with the authors' experience as psychologists and educators, to create a useful tool for the implementation of social, educational, and therapeutic interventions for the healthy social development of children and adolescents.

Belonging: Learning to feel safe in the world

In my experience, the behaviour of adolescents who struggle with school or relationships can often be traced back to early difficulties with healthy attachment and belonging. In The Circle of Courage model, belonging and attachment extends beyond attachment to parents alone, and includes the wider group of all adults within society, who become role models to children in everything they do. In traditional indigenous culture the sense of belonging is extended beyond parents into

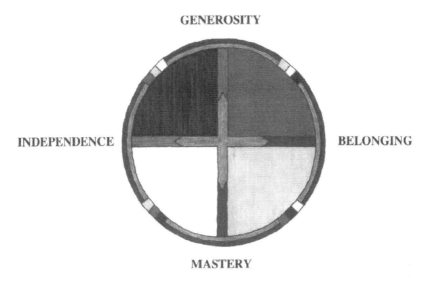

GENEROSITY

INDEPENDENCE

BELONGING

MASTERY

Figure 1 The Circle of Courage (Brendtro, Brokenleg, & Van Brockern, 1990)

the wider circle of extended family, tribe, culture, and ecological context. Mutual respect and concern for the others is central within most indigenous cultures and this respect extends to include, animals, plants and all of nature; a systemic world-view that is now growing in WEIRD culture, along with increased ecological awareness and concern. The Circle of Courage model therefore identifies the primary need for humans to belong, both socially and ecologically and how a loss of a healthy sense of belonging can lead to the pursuit of "artificial belonging", thus leading to an overdependence and craving for affect that we see in attachment disorders, a craving for a feeling of attachment at any cost (Brendtro, Brokenleg, & Van Brockern, 1990). In this section of the developmental wheel a strong sense of belonging is seen as a basic and primary human need.

Mastery: Inhabiting our bodies in the physical world

Adolescents who have experienced emotional disruptions in their early lives often find classroom education very difficult, since they cannot keep their bodies calm and have a constant need to move around. In the Circle of Courage model, Mastery describes the acquisition of the physical and social skills needed to function in a social group. The primary mastery in children is of their body in crawling, standing, and running, and later in adolescents the mastery of the complex emotions that are required for socialization.

In an education designed to just achieve academic success, physical skills and experiential education can be undervalued and may be considered less important than cognitive academic skills. However, it is likely that both body based learning and physical activity, which have the effect of releasing endorphins and reinforces a sense of belonging and joy, can enhance academic capability. In my experience of working with troubled adolescents the process of learning through the body has been very helpful because it aids the process of overcoming disruptive dissociation that is linked to attachment difficulties.

Independence: Taking responsibility for ourselves

Europeans who escaped to the "New World" of the Americas, and brought with them a culture of obedience that was formed by centuries of social oppression in Europe, were amazed to find that obedience was not part of indigenous American culture (Miller, 1955). According to Brendtro, Brokenleg, and Van Brockern (1990), traditional Native American culture placed a high value on personal autonomy and this began at a very early age, as children were encouraged and supported to develop their own sense of autonomy and control. Psychologist Abram Maslow, who developed his famous model of The Hierarchy of Needs, studied the indigenous Black Foot Indians child rearing practices. He observed how children were left to struggle with difficulties on their own and how their self-esteem was strengthened as a result (Maslow, 1971).

Generosity: Learning to be a generative adult

According to Brendtro, Brokenleg, and Van Brockern (1990) the most respected quality indigenous culture had was not the acquisition of wealth, but the ability to be able to give away to those in need. The Arctic explorer Peter Freuchen (1961) describes a dog sled journey he made over the Greenland icecap in the late 1950s with an indigenous Inuit guide. After months of grueling travel, running out of food, falling down a crevasse, losing sled dogs, and barely escaping with their lives, he recounts that when they arrived exhausted and starving back in the village, his Inuit companion pulled out a small pouch of tobacco and casually offered it to the first villages they met asking if they wanted a smoke, he had saved it specifically for this occasion (Freuchen 1961). This example fits with Brendtro, Brokenleg, and Van Brockern (1990) and Music's (2014) belief that altruism is the ultimate resource for coping with life's conflicts and in reaching out to help others we diminish the preoccupation with the self and reinforce a deeper sense of belonging or attachment within our community.

Building an outer attachment container

The Circle of Courage model recognizes that the creation of healthy attachment relationships in young people is enhanced by a supportive social ecology and by the creation of prosocial education and therapeutic environments. The model focuses initially on the environment required for the building of healthy attachment relationships, where these have not been developed in early life. Poor attachment experiences can result in *relationship reluctance*, where early experiences are perpetuated by a retreat into the virtual world, substance abuse, youth offending behaviour, or sexual promiscuity (Brendtro, Brokenleg, & Van Brockern, 1990).

Fragmentation of supportive social forms in WEIRD culture is detrimental to the capacity for youth to build positive and resilient attachment relationships of their own (Brendtro, Mitchel, & McCall, 2009). Where families are struggling with cross-generational social difficulties, young people build social groups amongst their peers or through social media sites, which can result in alienation between generations. Therefore parents and teachers tend to pathologize and fear adolescent behaviours that they do not understand. This alienation and distrust of adolescents is a relatively new cultural phenomenon, in the context of our indigenous historical perspective, and can result in young people not being given enough responsibility by the adults around them to fully mature.

In their book, *Deep Brain Learning: Pathways to Potential with Challenging Youth*, Brendtro, Mitchel, and McCall (2009) show how developments in neuroscience supports the idea of creating brain friendly learning environments for traumatized youth. These brain friendly learning experiences do not trigger the more primitive, deep brain response to perceived threats, and works best where the learning is experiential, non-threatening, and socially inclusive. A non-traumatizing learning environment therefore encourages the gradual development of an internal locus of control and self-agency. This is less likely when the learning environment is threatening and control is imposed by external restrictions and limitations (Brendtro, Mitchel, & McCall, 2009).

Building an inner attachment container

Essentially, the Circle of Courage model can be understood within the context of the triune brain (MacLean, 1990), as well as incorporating aspects of Bessel Van der Kolk's idea that the brain is primarily "an organ of attachment", that we continually learn our emotional regulation from those around us (Van der Kolk, 2014).

The oldest part of the brain, the reptilian brain, reacts in response to potential threats automatically and is primarily a motor function, allowing us to get away from unsafe situations. The limbic system of the brain, that wraps around the reptilian brain and regulates this flight and fight response through the amygdala, is based on previously established patterns of response to what might be dangerous. However, the neocortex, which surrounds the whole brain, has the capacity to over ride primitive fear reflexes in the limbic system and reptilian brain.

In healthy development the neocortex can also read and understand our own emotional responses and make decisions that ensure our own wellbeing. However, this capacity of self-control is late to develop in traumatized young people. The identification and function of these brain areas are now well known to neuroscience and integrative psychotherapy, but the Circle of Courage provides a developmental sequence, which can be used to understand developmental delay often experienced by young people considered to be youth at risk.

While obedience models of education and social care focus on compliance to social rules, the Circle of Courage focuses on the primary need for a sense of attachment and belonging, along with the embodiment of skills to master unhelpful impulses, in order to achieve independence and self-agency.

While the Circle of Courage model provides a useful neurological developmental map, it is also a useful guide for teams working with young people in order to create well thought out social and psychoeducational care plans that include the socioecological context of psychological health.

The Four Shields; an Intrapsychic nature based developmental wheel

The School of Lost Borders based in California, have spent more than thirty years training people to work with vision fast and rites of passage, use a nature based development wheel called The Four Shields (see Figure 2). This tool is similar to The Circle of Courage, but here the four qualities or shields are used to understand inner psyche states or soul qualities that can also be recognized in nature (Foster & Little, 1998a).

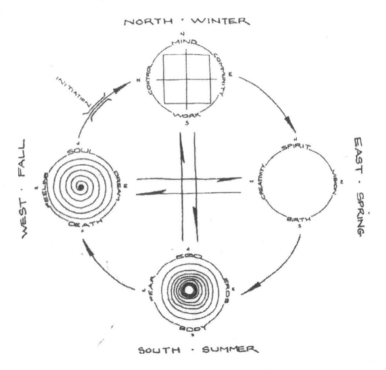

Figure 2 The Four Shields (Foster & Little, 1998a, p. 25)

I first met with Steven Foster and Meredith Little when they arrived in my hometown to give a workshop and I went to meet them, knowing only their names and their reputation as the founders of The School of Lost Borders. I was immediately struck by their relaxed authenticity. Steven Foster was a teacher of humanities and romantic poetry at the University of San Francisco in the 1960s. When he became involved in campus politics, as a supporter of student's rights, he was fired from his job along with other faculty members. Retreating into the Nevada desert to embrace his losses, he returned with a determination to create a contemporary nature based rite of passage for young people moving into adulthood, and so began to create experiential programmes for young people in the desert. In 1973 he met Meredith Little when they worked as partners on an all-night shift at Marin County Suicide Prevention Center in California and they went on to develop and found The School of Lost Borders.

Foster and Little's work drew on a wide range of both academic and indigenous teachings to create a pan cultural rite of passage that was not aligned to any particular spiritual tradition or path. They developed the Four Shields after working with a Native American teacher who taught them that this image is said to have originated in South America and had been passed on by word of mouth. Like the Circle of Courage their Four Shields is based on the solar cross and cardinal points, which move into each other developmentally, clockwise or sun wise round the wheel. This image also shows the two, North/South and East/West polarities that can be worked with through balancing the shields around the centre. The model also has a fractal nature, in which each directional quadrant has four sub qualities based on the four qualities of the whole, as illustrated in Figure 2.

Foster and Little (1998a) explain, the symbol is known as The Four Shields because the four aspects of nature, the East, South, West, and North, were also considered to be shields or defenses within this ancient indigenous psychology. These four inner qualities of the psyche or soul can also be found in nature and appear to be intimately connected at the imaginal level, that Foster (1998a) describes as the "self thus". The Four Shields also mark a point at the northwest of the wheel as initiation, the passage from the adolescent qualities of the West to the adult qualities of the North (Foster & Little, 1998a). Like the Circle of Courage the Four Shields are represented by the archetypal colours: Gold, Red, Black, and White. These colours appear in some European fairy tales, often as specific markers of particular stages of development within a journey or narrative, for example in the stories of Iron John and Snow White (Bly, 1990).

The imaginal qualities of the shields

The East shield: vision, birth, creativity, and spirit

The question that might be asked here is: *What aspect of my life is waiting to manifest?* And so the image of the golden rising sun represents the emergent potential of both the new day and beginning of the season of spring. This relates to the intuitive or spiritual vision of what might develop. The East shield therefore represents what is yet to be manifested in our lives. It is the quality of potential that can be recognized in the germination of the seeds in springtime, and is represented in the psyche as future visions and emergent potential.

The South shield: Eros, body, fear, and ego

The question that might be asked here is: *Where do I embrace joy and play in my life?* And the south shield corresponds to the season of summer and the colour red. This is the next stage of seasonal progress, which is characterized by the process of growth and manifestation, which we see in rapid plant growth and the reproductive period in the life cycle of animals. Summer shows the potential of the spring when it is most fully manifested. The south shield therefore represents the period in the human life cycle of childhood, characterized by joyful physicality, innocence, and impulsiveness, unrestricted by the complex emotions and social constraints of adolescence and adulthood.

The West shield: dreams, death, feeling, and soul

The question that might be asked here is: *What aspects of my life are dying away?* For that reason the West shield corresponds to the colour Black and the season of autumn, which marks the time of decay and fruit production in plants. Autumn is the time of contraction and return, furthermore an acknowledgement of the limitations of growth and the importance of the return to the earth. This shield in the human developmental cycle represents turning inward and introspection, characteristic of adolescence. This is a time often accompanied by deep feelings that mark the end of childhood and preparation of adulthood. It is a time of acknowledgement of the importance of dying within the cycle of the nature, and the need arises for the psyche to face the realities of both physical and psychological death.

The North shield: community, work, control, and mind

The question that might be asked here is: *Where do I embrace responsibly and care for others in my life?* The North shield is depicted in white representing the winter season. This is the most contracted period of nature's seasons, with a focus on survival until spring returns. The North shield therefore represents the adult phase of the life cycle, a time of self-responsibility and generosity to others. It is thought to be the most important shield with a focus on the role of adults supporting others, thus securing a safe future for children and adolescents in the community.

The hero's journey; reading human life as an imaginal narrative

Foster (1998a, 1998b) spent years researching story and myths in relation to these four shields. He became convinced that the archetypal stages of the shields were more widely known and were even represented in European fairy tales. The idea that we can use archetypal myths and stories to make sense of life's events has been previously explored and documented in detail by Joseph Campbell. Campbell was a mythologist who described an archetypal or imaginal pattern of story that he called the hero's journey, a mono-myth that he saw repeated in Egyptian, Greek, and Christian mythologies (Campbell, 1993).

Foster combined the images of The Four Shields and Campbell's idea of the hero's journey to create a contemporary developmental narrative of the passage from adolescence into adulthood. He recognized the "extreme ordeal" that often appears in European myths as a psychological and spiritual rite of passage (Foster 1998a, 1998b).

The idea of the mono-myth and the hero's journey was popularized by a student of Campbell's work, George Lucas, who famously used the hero's journey as the basis for the story behind the Star Wars films. According to Fosters map, this journey begins in the East, with new birth and childhood innocence and the secure base of a healthy attachment. The journey continues to the South with the learning of skills required to engage in the physical world. In the next stage of adolescence it continues in the West, with the ordeal of facing some type of psychological death involving a descent into the underworld. Finally arriving at the north with the capacity to become a supportive and generative adult.

The Poet Robert Bly outlines this journey in his book about the fairy tale of Iron John, where the young boy has to leave his home after releasing a wild man that his parents have captured and caged in the courtyard of the castle. The boy becomes apprenticed to the wild man before setting off to make his own way in the world and passing through a time of despair. During this time he takes on the lowest job in the neighbouring King's castle, clearing out the ashes from the kitchen fireplace. The boy then begins his ascent into adulthood through a series of dangerous trials until he is recognized for his gifts and is eventually honoured by the King (Bly, 1990).

Bill Plotkin's Soulcentric and Ecocentric developmental wheel

Bill Plotkin depth psychologist, ecotherapist, and founder of the Animus Valley Institute, acknowledges The School of Lost Borders and the Four Shields model in the development of a nature based development mapping tool that he calls the Soulcentric/Ecocentric stages of human development (Figure 3).

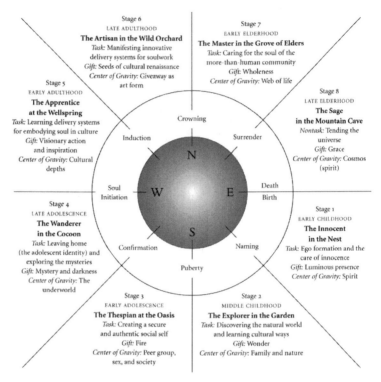

The Eight Soulcentric/Ecocentric Stages of Human Development
From Nature and the Human Soul © Bill Plotkin (New World Library, 2008)
soulcraft@animas.org

Figure 3 Bill Plotkin's Soulcentric/Ecocentric developmental wheel (Plotkin, 2008)

In his book *Soulcraft*, Plotkin (2003) describes how in the past psycho-spiritual development paths have been described in two opposite ways: as an ascendant path or descendent path. The ascendant path is oriented upwards, towards the Gods and away from the earth, and can be seen in some aesthetic religions such as Buddhist and Christian practices, a path which is geared towards enlightenment or heavenly transcendence.

The descendant path in contrast was oriented downwards, towards the earth, and can be seen in some myths and fairy tales where the task is to descend into the underworld to retrieve a special gift. This is the essence of the hero's journey. The descendent journey has been used as an image by depth psychologists like Carl Jung and James Hillman and recognizes the importance of the mastery of the physicality of the body and the developmental value of the "extreme ordeal", and encountering perhaps an aspect of the unconscious. Plotkin acknowledges the importance of both these aspects of psychological health in his Eco–Soul Centric Wheel, the descent from childhood and the ascent to adulthood, through the process of soul initiation and the discovery of the wellspring of our adult life.

Though this Soul Centric Developmental Wheel begins with the four cardinal points, Plotkin (2008) has developed it further to recognize eight stages of development. He describes these stages as being unavoidable psycho-ecological phases, like the seasons, and are not externally determined by cultural, or parental belief, religious pressure, or state authority; they are parts of an emergent healthy identity. Plotkin also makes the distinction between the ego, that enables us to function in the world, and the soul, that is called to become embodied in the world, and discovered or remembered through the spontaneous insights that often occur in initiatory processes, and are then confirmed on one or more occasions by revelatory experiences.

A healthy adulthood, as described by Plotkin, involves "Soul centric" stages of development where it is possible to consciously recognize and embody the uniqueness of an individual's psyche or soul. He calls this our "Eco-psychological niche" in the world, a unique mythopoeic and ecological identity, and is independent of our family, and our social or culturally determined context. He contrasts this to our "Egocentric" development in WEIRD culture where we choose our own identity or it is given and sometimes imposed on us by others. This identity is then orientated towards our material and social status and therefore any emergent psycho-spiritual challenges tend to be pathologized, avoided, or pass unrecognized. Unfortunately, working with the imaginal in nature and valuing nature based initiatory rites of passage, does not fit neatly into contemporary WEIRD cultures' educational or psychotherapeutic paradigms.

Like the Circle of Courage Wheel, Plotkin's Soul Centric Developmental Wheel recognizes the primary importance of attachment and belonging within his eight stages of development. Stages 1 and 2 that include *The Innocent in the nest* and *The Explorer in the garden* are imaginal descriptions of the value of early innocence and the importance of family and social and ecological context. The following stages 3 and 4, *The Thespian at the oasis* and *The Wanderer in the cocoon*, acknowledges and identifies the difficulties that adolescents experience after leaving the comfort and support of childhood. They represent the dangerous and alluring call to descend; the underworld journey in search of a more authentic sense of self. Finally, stages five through to eight describe the qualities of a path that can lead to a generative adulthood and elderhood; the journey of surrendering to old age and death.

However, Plotkin's Soulcentric and WEIRD cultures Egocentric developmental narratives part company with the transition to stage five *The Apprentice at the wellspring*, at "Soul Initiation" in the West. Although we are familiar with the role of initiation from myths and fairy tales, where the hero receives a transformational experience after a life-threating ordeal, we do not have sophisticated psychological or educational language to describe this in WEIRD culture. At this stage the WEIRD Egocentric worldview has come to the edge of the road map, soul initiation has become a subjugated narrative and the search for and discovery of our personal psycho-spiritual wellspring is not widely discussed by most teachers, ecologists, or psychologists.

One notable exception however is found in the work of James Hillman who describes some aspects of this journey in his book *The Soul's Code*, where he provides examples of how this "Calling" and subsequent "Soul encounter" have shaped human biographies (Hillman, 1997). Without the imaginal language required to negotiate the passage of soul initiation of early adulthood; this stage can become a search for fulfillment through the acquisition of material goods and power, which although important, never fully satisfies deeper psychological need that Plotkin describes as stage 5, *The Apprentice at the wellspring*.

Perhaps the consequences of the inability to pass beyond stage four, if seen from a mental health perspective, offers some insight into aspects of adolescent depression, self-harm, and suicidal ideation, and the powerful gravitation pull towards darkness in adolescent subcultures. The experience of a pull towards a symbolic psychological death, without adequate imaginal language can become too literal, and is tragically mistaken as a desire for a physical death. This perspective might provide valuable insight into adolescent self-harming behaviour, as well as the phenomena of school shootings and adolescent suicide.

Rudolf Steiner's Imaginal map: head, heart, and hands

Having trained as a Rudolf Steiner teacher and studied his writing for more than twenty years, it's interesting that much of his work is only now being confirmed by research. However Steiner's work and language is difficult to understand and, because of its esoteric nature, cannot usually be useful in academic research. Nevertheless, a study of the practices based on his work (biodynamic agriculture, medicine, and Waldorf education) can reveal something of its implicit epistemology.

It seems likely that Rudolf Steiner and Gregory Bateson shared a similar epistemology and hermeneutic, or way of reading the world; both acknowledged the alchemical studies of Goethe as a starting point for their enquiry (Bateson, 1979; Steiner, 2000). Although Steiner died in 1925 it's possible that if he was alive today he might call himself an ecopsychologist (Van Evera-Roth, 2002), since much of his work pointed to the systemic links between psyche and nature. Steiner suggested ways of enhancing healthy development through connecting natural and social environments, while emphasizing the importance of social context and contact with nature within education. These ideas are now supported by the work of Bird (2007) and Music (2014) who describe the calming effects of contact with nature and the influence of prosocial environments respectively. He suggested a three-fold nature of the mind, human organization, and the natural world, long before the now well established idea of the triune brain (MacLean, 1990).

This simple imaginal development map suggested by Steiner can also be seen in the work of Dutch psychiatrist Bernard Lievegoed (1946) and others who work with this model of the human body, as a vertical polarity between the thinking processes in the head and the digestive processes in the body, mediated by the feeling processes of the heart. In recent work that understands the effect of traumatic experiences in children's lives, there is recognition of the value of learning emotional self-regulation by working with the body through a "bottom up" approach to education and therapy (Van der Kolk, 2014). This is characteristic of Steiner's education model where body movement, and art and craft are considered developmentally important. This model that replicates the triune brain reoccurs throughout Steiner's ideas on human development and is also a valuable tool in identifying patterns in forms and processes in nature.

As well as describing links between nature and mind, Steiner also promoted a systemic rather than a reductionist approach to the study of nature, an approach that has been further developed by biologists such as Andreas Suchantke (2009, 2001). Suchantke explored deep patterns in the forms of animal and plants that mirror some of the characteristics of the triune brain and seem to show links between both psychological and ecological systems.

Recognition of the socially constructed nature of WEIRD thinking can therefore allow the questioning of strongly held cultural beliefs and open the way to the possibility of holding other views and multiple perspectives. The nature based developmental maps discussed in this chapter that have their basis in indigenous models of human developmental have, in some cases, been in use for 15,000 years. These models are based on imaginal narratives and are informed by non-conceptual and experiential learning and so could easily be dismissed as irrelevant. However, the systemic nature of these models describes patterns of change and emergence, not linear processes of development, and these can be observed both in nature and human growth.

From a meta perspective these nature based developmental maps provide potentially useful images to work with, where contemporary models of education and mental health appear to have become over mechanistic to a point where they no longer seem useful. An imaginal perspective can provide complimentary insights where formulation has become trapped in pleromal and reductionist thinking. Likewise, these models are examples of systemic processes that recognize the importance of the links between nature and the human mind in ecotherapy and ecopsychology practice. And it is for this reason that natured based maps are useful models when working with a soulcentric approach that explore imaginal aspects of human development and nature based rites of passage, not usually recognized by an egocentric approach. The maps therefore help to make sense of experiences of imaginal soul encounters that are common during vision fasts or vision quests, but are difficult to describe in academic language. Working with these nature based developmental maps and wheels is an effective way of expanding our thinking about nature and mental health and challenges the socially constructed borders of WEIRD culture.

Chapter 6

Soul encounter beyond the borders of language

In the early 1970s a reawakening of interest occurred in the value of nature based rites of passage for adolescents, a practice that had seemed essential to the cultural integrity of most indigenous societies. Around this time Steven Foster and Meredith Little began wilderness rites of passage work in California and went on to found The School of Lost Borders. The Jungian analyst Louise Carus Mahdi also became interested in researching rites of passage and along with Foster and Little they later collaborated as editors on two books, collated writings on rites of passage, and gathered a selection of rich material on the importance of initiation for youth and the different initiatory paths (Mahdi, Christopher, & Meade, 1996; Mahdi, Foster, & Little, 1987). In their book, *Crossroads: The Quest for Contemporary Rites of Passage*, Mahdi, Christopher, and Meade (1996), formulated the connection between adolescent development and rites of passage. They also showed how this process might be recreated and resourced to make them relevant to contemporary culture.

The search for a contemporary nature based rites of passage

The School of Lost Borders based in a Californian desert landscape, works with a form of vision quest learnt directly from a Native American indigenous elder. Foster and Little further developed this method, that they call vision fast, in order to facilitate rites of passage for those adolescents and adults who were wanting to mark important changes in their lives, as well as learning how nature can be a co-facilitator in their experience. These vision quests or vision fasts involved four days of solo time in nature and used the Four Shields model of human development, and worked with an explicit assumption that nature could be a mirror and teacher for the psyche. In an attempt to create a "pan cultural rite of passage" that could be accessible to any race, religion, culture or gender, The School of Lost Borders removed most of the culturally specific aspects of the experience in order to simplify the process down to its bare bones. After many years of work the essence of the process was encapsulated in a four day and night period of solo time in nature without food, company, or shelter, where important life transitions or questions can be acknowledged and marked using self generated ritual.

Ritual solo fasting is quite different from the practice of survival skills in nature, such as bush craft, since the focus is not on survival, but is about consciously inviting nature into a relationship. This can create an opening for a deeper imaginal awareness of the connection between the participants and nature, generating a channel for communicating with the natural world, with the animals, plants, rocks, and even the wind. This approach takes the experience well beyond the language and belief structures of WEIRD culture and is maybe difficult to grasp without having a direct personal experience. Solo time is less about surviving and more about thriving in the other-than-human world; it's about stepping into a different way of being with nature that is rare in the Western world.

Having spent much of my early life trying to immerse myself in nature and wilderness, I did not expect to learn very much from camping out in the woods for four days on my first vision fast. How wrong I was. The vision fast is a visceral and yet mythic journey in real time, a descent into and return from the underworld, where the boundaries between nature and psyche become porous, and yet it has a beautiful quality that is similar to the all-absorbing experience of childhood symbolic play. Self-generated ritual involves stepping out of conscious control of our normal everyday environment and inviting a relationship with nature, as a sentient "other" to unfold as it may.

This experience appears to open an intersubjective dialogue between nature and psyche and can lead to profound and insights that have a quality of the psychotic, but are not by their nature, necessarily pathologic or negative. The experience can have a lasting and transformative emotional and behavioural impact, and as such can be thought of as the visionary aspect of the vision quest, although the experience is better described as an *imaginal* communication, through dreams or life affirming breakthrough images, voices, thoughts, or encounters with nature.

After four days and nights of continuous exposure to nature, participants on the vision fast often find the return to companionship and re-engagement with the human made world particularly difficult. Although this gradually reduces with the introduction of food and company, they can be highly emotional, sensitive, and vulnerable. The return stage, or *reincorporation* is supported by the sharing of the story from the solo time in nature, in image or narrative, so that this experience can be personally integrated. This can happen through the retelling and the use of a type of externalization, particularly where the story is retold as a third person narrative.

This process is not the same as externalization that is used in narrative therapy to help gain understanding, but simply a witnessing of the embodied imaginal experience of the solo fast, without needing to make sense of it, or engaging in psychotherapy. The mirroring of the story *imaginally* in images and metaphors, seems to communicate directly with the body and implicit memory, and supports the emotional affirmation of the participant's experience.

Although the vision quest experience is undoubtedly psychotherapeutic, it is very different from psychotherapy. Bill Plotkin (2003) makes the distinction between the *Egocentric* focus of psychotherapy that can help us function less painfully and more successfully in the context of our family or culture, and the *soulcentric* focus of *soul craft* work, such as vision quests. Plotkin (2003) believes that vision quests or vision fasts have the capacity to break down our ego defenses and open us up to letting go of an egocentric worldview, thus inviting recognition of our own unique contribution and its manifestation in our community and culture. Foster and Little told me that the traditional teaching about the experience of an imaginal "vision" was that it should not be talked about but just "manifest on the earth for the people to see" (Personal communication, 2001).

Martin Jordan (2015), who studied and wrote about the use of outdoor therapeutic methods, made it clear that vision quests are not therapy that is aimed to make you feel better, but is a way of breaking away from the support of old and obsolete beliefs and habits, and as such, can make life more authentic, though maybe more difficult.

Even without facilitation, a natural process similar to vision quest appears to occur quite spontaneously after about three days exposure to the natural world. Robert Greenway writes that after a short time away in nature, when humans leave behind their daily world worries and begin to think and dream in a more archetypal language, something profound happens; some times know as the *wilderness effect*. In fact he suggests that our culture is "only four days deep" (Greenway, 1995, p. 129), meaning it only takes about four days in the wilderness for the process of leaving civilization behind and to connect deeply with wild nature. It is even possible to create a self-generated vision quest just by spending time alone and fasting in nature. However, The School of Lost Borders model of this work contains some implicit practices that can powerfully enhance what appears to be an essentially natural process. When engaging in this work, the best way to describe this experience of approaching nature, using a more psychological language, is "relational". In this way nature is being approached as a respected sentient other, as in the relationship between a therapist and their client.

This work is greatly benefited if participants have built trust in the support of the guides, who are able to hold the individuals of the group in mind and ensure that the whole process is safe. In this way the guides can create an invisible attachment container for the group, which enables participants to feel safe, physically, emotionally, and spiritually. This happens most effectively where the groups are carefully supported during the preparation phase and the guides work from their own integrity of professional practice and experience. This is particularly important during the return phase when participants come back from the fast with their stories; the incorporation and embodiment of these experiences is a slow process, sometimes taking up to a year to be digested. This period is alluded to in myths and fairy tales and is often described as "a year and a day" a significant and complete natural cycle of change or one cycle of the solar cross.

Piercing the heart

On the last night of my vision fast with The School of Lost Borders, I prepared for my nightlong vigil and found a place on a high rocky outcrop facing the East. I wrapped myself in my sleeping bag and waited for the dawn. The stars turned like a great clock, hours passed, and finally the eastern sky brightened and as dawn broke my heart felt like it began to sing. As this feeling rose in me, a tiny wren flew in and landed on a rock less than six feet away, it looked towards the East and began to sing towards the rising sun. The wren and I looked at each other and we exchanged an unspoken acknowledgment and then she continued the serious task of singing up the sun.

I am an adoptee and was adopted at a young age and did not meet my birthmother again until I was forty. I had arranged to travel to California for one month to attend this experiential training in wilderness rites of passage, just prior to making contact with her. The training culminated in a vision fast, and my mother had promised to send me a letter giving details of my birth family before I went out on the fast. On the second week of the training, Tuesday 11 September 2001 we heard about the attack on the twin towers in New York and all planes were grounded, my letter never arrived so I went out into the desert without it.

I spent my time alone in the high desert of the Inyo Mountains surrounded by rocky pine forest and by night a vast canopy of stars. At the end of each day I made my way down from my camp to the *buddy pile*. A stone we had chosen on the first day as a place to leave signs and messages, so that my buddy and I could let each other know that we were ok, without meeting up. On the last day, thinking I had completed all the tasks of the fast, I walked down to the buddy pile one more time and there, on the stone, was the promised letter from my mother. I read it and felt like, some of the old armour I used to protect myself was blown away and I sat down on the ground for a while to recover. As I walked back up the hill to my camp I kicked a strange old piece of metal that looked like a burst copper water pipe. I was told later that this area of old Native American sacred ground had been used for target practice by fighter planes in World War II, the object I picked up was the remains of an exploded amour-piercing shell. Receiving the letter after four days fasting in nature had a powerful emotional impact, and the process had been mirrored in an imaginal metaphor in nature by finding the physical remains of the armour-piercing shell.

The process of reconnecting to feelings that we have forgotten can be emotionally overwhelming and remembering our ancient relationship with nature can be a challenging process. Deep ecologist Joanna Macy believed that there is an urgent need to "reconnect" to nature's complexity, suggesting one way to change our modern perception is through the experience of grief of what we have lost and might lose in the future (Macey & Brown, 1998). The Jungian analyst Robert Romanyshyn also believes, from his own experience of grief, that loss has the power to open a connection to nature and to change our limited modernist perception.

Vision fast and psychotherapy

The work pioneered by Foster and Little (1998a, 1998b) has now grown through their training programmes to inform other nature based rites of passage work throughout the world. Each person who undergoes this journey brings back a potentially life changing experience that is uniquely their own, but the stories they bring back often share themes of being deeply reconnected to nature as well as profound personal healing.

The relationship between the vision quest experience and clinical psychotherapy is yet to be fully explored and although vision quest is certainly therapeutic it is very different from psychotherapy. In fact, I believe the two processes are complimentary; those working as vision quest or vision fast guides can benefit from an experience of psychotherapy and psychotherapists have much to gain from the experience of vision quest. However, it seems more work is needed in the development of a common language. Sardello (2008) suggests that two separate processes were carefully differentiated by the Gnostic alchemists "the lesser work" and "the Great work" (p. 127). While, the lesser work included the process of balancing our interpersonal lives in a cultural context, that today we might recognize as similar to psychotherapy. The Great work involved the Soulcentric/Ecocentric task of engaging with the soul's unique relationship with the natural world.

For many year, research into neuropathways of autonomic fear responses linked to childhood trauma indicated that such behaviours were impossible to alter through psychotherapy. However more recent developments in neuroscience have discovered that it is possible to alter fear responses in patients who had experienced trauma. This can be done through a process called *memory reconsolidation* and showed that these previous deeply fixed neuropathways can be changed and permanently erased (Ecker, Ticic, & Hulley, 2012). The process involves the emotional activation of the original specific traumatic experience, while simultaneously experiencing a contradictory and positive mismatching perspective. This activates the creation of new neuropathways and eliminates symptoms at their roots. This is one possible neurological framing for the effectiveness of transformational wilderness rites of passage experiences and a fruitful area for further research.

A study by Melissa Kohner on the effectiveness of a wilderness rites of passage experience involving a vision fast, explored the transformative function of symbols for a group of individuals (Kohner, 2012). The study drew on the ideas of Carl Jung, that symbols have the capacity to mediate between the "ego"; our sense of who we believe we are, and the "self"; a larger totality or wholeness that includes the unconscious part of the psyche or soul. Kohner considered the process of initiation as the "embodiment of the archetype of death and rebirth" (Kohner, 2012, p. 44.), and the breakdown of the boundary between the ego and the self. She describes how nature based rites of passage are different from modern day social rites of passage, such as graduations and retirement. These, she says, do not necessarily involve the internal psychological process of ego transcendence that can occur in a vision fast. In her study Kohner interviewed eight individuals between the ages of thirty-eight and seventy who recounted their own experience of a vision fast. The length of time between the original experience and the interview varied from two weeks to thirty-three years.

All participants, however, reported feeling profoundly impacted by the symbolic experience during and after their vision fast. The descriptions of the participants' symbolic experience also shared a number of characteristic qualities:

- The experience took them by surprise and demanded their attention.
- There was a strong emotional charge and the symbol was outside of their conscious creation.
- The experience was meaningful, but in most case the meaning was not immediately clear.

(Kohner, 2012, p. 84)

Kohner's study showed that the symbolic experiences encountered during the participants' wilderness rites of passage often occurred in response to previous significant loss and disillusionment in their lives. Though the symbols were often surprising, they demanded their attention to address personal core psychological issues. Engagement with these symbolic messages therefore resulted in participants confronting their own redundant patterns of behaviour. Ultimately these symbols became psychologically integrated by participants, resulting in an expanded sense of self and greater levels of satisfaction and growth in their personal lives and careers (Kohner, 2012).

Despite increasing interest in the value of a deeper connection with nature based rites of passage and initiation processes, they are still not widely researched or understood. This can result in attempts to copy and revive old indigenous or shamanic practice, creating a kind of nostalgia for a past connection with nature that is now forever closed off and superseded by a scientific understanding of nature and mental health. My experience of work with vision fast and soul craft work is that this approach has the potential for revealing areas of individual personal development that might need attention. This work also has the effect of opening up a more reflective and soul centric worldview, which would include a deeper and more spiritual connection with nature.

From a systemic perspective soul craft and vision fast work in nature can be a powerful way of bringing about new reflective insights that can result in transformation and the "re-storying" of old reoccurring narratives that have proved resistant to change and as a result led to missed life opportunities. For this reason the work could be a useful additional therapeutic approach when working with adolescents and adults struggling with unresolved issues that prove resistant to change, and where nature can sometimes provide a safe space and new insight.

I believe this way of working with individuals – adults or adolescents – is also helpful for those wishing to find a deeper connection with nature, and provides a framework for a more systemic approach that links ecology and human activity.

The relationship between humans and land has a long history involving hunting and cultivation for food and more recently for recreation purposes and conservation as other areas are protected from human influence in national parks and wildlife reserves. However, the therapeutic value of soul work within nature that can be experienced during soul encounter such as vision fast is less well understood. This is an important future area for discussion between wilderness and soul craft guides, teachers, therapists, and landowners, in order to establish areas of land that can be specifically designated for the safe practice of nature based soul centric ecopsychotherapy.

Participants' voices

Testimonials of personal experiences of vision fast

The Sinai Desert Mandala

A male participant in a facilitated vision fast in the Sinai desert in Egypt including four day and night solo time

I went into the vision quest with a strong sense of needing to shift particular patterns around insecurity in the presence of others, inwardly seeking approval, inability to stay confidently with my own thread. I was in my late twenties, an apprentice on a biodynamic farm and I had a feeling of being on the brink of adulthood but somewhere unable to step into what I perceived to be "adulthood" which I associated with self-determination, confidence, resilience etc.

~

In the desert, when I was fasting, I built an elaborate circular mandalic form of some scale, which I planned to gradually build over the days alone, each daily stage having some ritual significance to the stages of vision quest. In the centre I built a fire every night and from here danced, sung, and watched the incredible desert night skies.

~

I had chosen my place for the vision quest to be a small cave in the curve of a natural Amphitheatre shaped outcrop of rock. It was open at one end, facing out to the northwest and this seemed like an ideal location. Once the vision quest began, I soon realised why the cave existed in the curved wall of the "amphitheatre". It was hollowed out by sand that was whipped up into a vortex by the wind as it hit the curved walls of the rocky outcrop. I had entered my ritual space imagining that I had found an ideal little hollow with a great view, to find that every time the wind blew (which it did at night) I was cold and distinctly uncomfortable. Our guidance was that once we'd chosen our place we should try to stay with it and I felt that this was right but it challenged my picture of a kind of seamless, highly aesthetic ritual, one that I could share with others upon my return (and perhaps get approval?). I tried to improve my accommodation by using a tarpaulin to build a door to the cave entrance but it was all rather hopeless and it struck me that I have a need to be accommodated, to be safe, I felt very exposed. It gave me a sense of my own lack of safety with myself, that the reassurance I sought by others approval was something that I lacked in myself.

~

I stayed with my mandala building, grinding down sandstone of different colours and adding to the circle but on the third night I started to feel really strange; heightened, buzzing, confused, and nauseous, and eventually decided to head back to base camp. I collapsed at base camp with a violent stomach bug and found myself extremely ill, devoid of energy and drifting between sleeping and waking. I was reassured by the care of the group leaders and Bedouin guides; I recall them whispering nearby by the fire as they ate Ramadan breakfast at 3am together and a supportive hand regularly placed on me to check my condition.

~

I stayed in that state for the rest of the next day but then I was encouraged to go back to my place for the last night. The guide helped me back there, I remember feeling so supported and he left me there for the night. I don't recall much from that night, nor do I recall the walk back to base camp the next day. However, the group reflection that evening, as I sat in a Bedouin tent together with my fellow vision questers, remains vividly in me; I recall the night sky being unbelievably clear and each companion sharing from a place of sincerity, vulnerability, and deep respect for one and other.

~

I think the experience helped me to stand in my own shoes a bit more. Soon afterwards I took on the running and development of a farm and I met *many experiences with colleagues, which reflected my issues of seeking self-approval and finding personal resources of resilience and reassurance in myself.*

~

On reflection, my "grand plan" for the vision quest with the large scale sand mandala and rituals, which was trimmed down by the wholesale stomach bug which hit me on day three, helped me to loosen up a little around expected outcomes vs. the real outcomes. It touched very much into the space of my relationship with my father whom I experienced feelings of intense disappointment around during my period of recovery upon my return to England. I think the vision quest laid a path out to exploring this disappointment at various times in the following few years and to see my father's issues around approval in my own narrative and how this had played out in my young adult life.

~

So, the vision quest didn't change everything overnight but it set me on an orientation to these places which had been stuck and caused me lots of uncertainty and anxiety. In my twenties I'd had lots of problems with my belly, not serious but just lots of aches, bloating, and discomfort. When the violent sickness happened it came from a familiar place in a way, just much more intense and severe. I felt afterwards something had shifted in my belly and didn't suffer anything like as much subsequently in this area (although again I can't say it changed overnight, more of a slow gentle subsidence afterwards).

~

A few months after, I also met the love of my life (and now mother of my children) and I was better able to stay with my uncertainty in this scenario and move into living together. Looking back the vision quest was a threshold into the qualities of adulthood that I had imagined; confidence, resilience, self-determination – they didn't just spring up in me after the vision quest but I began to dialogue with myself about them and thus work with myself more openly with less crushing expectation.

~

Mountain incantation

A female participant in a facilitated vision fast in
southern Europe including four days and night solo

If I think of my experience of Vision Quest I see a white rock in sunshine. A beautiful big flat topped boulder with a tree growing right through it.

I feel the sun's great arc as it crosses the sky from dawn to dusk, and the sound of sheep bells in the distance coming closer and closer, a big rush of noise and activity as they pass by my rock, and the sound passing off into the distance until the next day when it will all happen again.

~

I look up to the distant head-topped mountain, which said "Seer" to me before I even settled into my space. I did not know what Seer meant, and neither did I know that a quester can expect to be given a name. And most of all, the mountain I was on, opening up when I fell upon the "incantation" that unlocked it. No less than ALL the Mother love that I had ever lacked being bestowed onto me.

~

These things filled out my life in every aspect, forming part of who I am, and still becoming. Nothing was ever the same again, and it lives on.

I came home with a "sound" which has remained with me for all the years that have passed since (more than twenty years), and continues to help me to find a sense of home, and focus in any situation.

~

My life is marked by Before and After V.Q.

Walking through Death Valley

A female participant in a facilitated vision fast in
California including four days and night solo

I wouldn't talk about it as a Vision "Quest" but as a Vision "Fast". The difference is important to me in that I did not go to the Inyo mountains for a "vision" but committed to a fast which I think, at the time, I expected to help me find ways to heal from much pain and sorrow carried over since childhood and teenage hood. Second time round was similar in that I mostly sought greater understanding of myself and that I wanted to mark the passage of the end of motherhood with a second fast.

~

I have done much and walked a whole range of different paths in order to understand myself better. The experience of the vision fast still ranks as the "best" in its soothing and transformational power.

The effect or outcome of the first vision fast was a sense of wholeness which I had never experienced before and which has stayed with me ever since. Of course, feeling or being "whole" meant that I had to learn to hold both my light and darkness together, as one. The "reincorporation" year which followed this first fast probably remains one of the most difficult years of my life in going through this process – who would enjoy facing and holding one's darkness – or "hugging" it – instead of ignoring it or escaping from it through addiction?

~

The effect of the second vision fast was a real ceremony of myself as a woman. It helped me honour the woman in me in ways that were both natural and also surprising. Whilst wholeness has emerged as the destination of the first fast's reincorporation time, 'tenderness' emerged as the next destination for me.

~

The general outcome of both vision fasts was an increasingly sense of merging with nature. Nature becoming my mother, my father, my guide, a source of great love and light. It triggered a devotion for the safeguarding of the earth and nature wherever I am or go that has only expanded with time since.

~

Both fasts also reaffirmed my faith in spirit through experiences, which I cannot explain in rational terms. The second fast gifted me with the experience of predictive visual vignettes in cloud formations for example. It is only now – three quarters into my second reincorporation year – that I can recognize that what I saw was predictive.

~

Each vision fast was transformational physically: I lost weight and felt much better in my body. My skin glowed and I had clearly "detoxed" in some form. It also helped emotionally: I returned to a place of peace – as an outcome of some form of "reconciliation" – first time around and experienced joy second time around.

~

Mentally, both fasts helped me review my life with nature mirroring whatever I questioned or pondered about. The mirroring provided me with many insights.

~

Spiritually, both fasts were marvellous. The second fast in particular. I walked through Death Valley with the spirit by my side and around me, and with the spirit in me. I received messages and held conversations with some of my ancestors.

~

The effect of both fasts was therefore unique, precious, and is still ongoing. Ways I had forgotten or had never experienced before I feel that each vision fast provided me with the means to redirect my life towards a more authentic way of being.

Suggested design criteria for holding a vision fast

- Staff need to be trained with well-established wilderness rites of passage training organizations
- Staff need to have had extensive personal experience of Soul craft work and their own vision fasts
- Staff on the team need to have appropriate knowledge/training in psychotherapy
- Rigorous, medical, psychological screening of participants
- Rigorous first aid, risk assessments, and evacuation procedures
- Careful psychological and practical preparation of participants for the experience including advice on equipment and first aid
- Instruction on *leave no trace* camping
- Appropriate insurance and staff police checks

- Permission and access to work in an extensive area of a relatively intact ecosystem for up to four days and nights, either forest, mountain, or desert
- In-depth knowledge of the land in terms of weather, human, and non-human dangers, including knowledge of history and trauma in the land.

Therapeutic soul centric and vision fast activities intentional or spontaneous

- Solo time in nature, static or walking in nature, and without food, shelter, or company (Foster & Little, 1998)
- Use of self-generated ritual or ceremony (Foster & Little, 1998)
- Engaging in preparation for the reality of [you own] death, practically or ritually – "dying practice"
- Speaking and listening in reflective council (Zimmerman & Coyle, 1996)
- Soul centric encounters with mythopoeic symbols in story, myth, and poetry (Plotkin 2003; Shaw, 2011)
- Working with deep imagery in dreams and psychotherapy (Plotkin, 2003)
- Working with synchronistic experiences and meaningful communication with the other than human world; animals, plants, rocks, and wind (Plotkin, 2003)
- Engagement in creating symbolic or soul centric art work, painting, music, dance, sculpture or craft, bodywork, and movement (Plotkin, 2003).

Qualitative data on wilderness experience

In a dissertation by Melissa Kohner six major themes arose that were considered to reflect the sequential stages that are characteristic of an archetypal intuition process (Kohner, 2012). These stages that were recorded in the interviews, are:

1 **Things fall apart**
My relationship was clearly dying and I wasn't willing to see that, but I kept trying to revive it. And my work, I was totally burnt out and I knew I had to leave but didn't have a good inspiration for where else I would go.

2 **Something needs to change**
Then I hear this voice this day as I was writing in my journal that said "if you don't do something about your life right now, you will live a long life, but your pilot light will be out" I just broke down, because I knew it meant I had to step up in some way I had not been stepping up.

3 **The experience of the symbol**
Each day in the morning this little butterfly would show up and it would fly around me. . .I had the experience that this butterfly and I were connected. . .I wanted it to land on my hand. I put my hand out each day and this happened lot and lots of times and it would not land. It would fly around really close but it would not land one me . . .so I got my drum out and I decide that I really need to be true to myself. I'd said "this is going to be really important", I was going to drum all the time, and I never drummed and I gotta take myself more seriously I started drumming. I had not drummed for more than ten seconds and this butterfly come flying in and landed right on my heart. Isn't that incredible? It just zoomed right into my heart and landed on my chest over my heart.

4 **Recognition**
I've had the notion of butterflies as symbolic of rebirth and trans-formation. An invitation to transform and get out of my cocoon.
It's an age thing too At my age I'm not going out rock climbing any-more. . .If I'm going to work as a guide, it's going to be a different way of working.

5 **Ego – Self axis – the tension between the old ego and new self**
A couple of my friends had told me before I left, they said, "I'm really looking forward to seeing you come back I think you'll be completely different" And I said "it's just a twelve-day fast. You

know, shit, I'll come back and I'll know some new things". But I came back and I was different. And it fucked up my life in some ways.

6   Ongoing dialog with the symbol

[Discussing the sale of the shared property after a divorce, some years after the fast]

I wanted to live here, and it would be nice to share it with her, but it really was my image [to buy the property]. I was able to actually pull the image of the butterfly back and say this is about being true to myself and I gotta quit being such a cry baby about circumstances, because actually I asked for this. I bought it. I wanted it.

Chapter 7

Patterns of systemic relationships in nature

In his seminal book on the Artic, Barry Lopez wrote about a journey he took in northern Canada together with biologists and research scientists who were studying the artic ecology. He records the perspective of the indigenous Inuit hunters and how their observations of nature differ from those of the scientists (Lopez, 1986). It is clear that Lopez straddles the divide between indigenous and scientific thinking. While he is well versed in reading academic papers, he also spent time with the Inuit, immersing himself in the landscape, walking slowly over the tundra, allowed him to be able to listen to the land in the same manner as the indigenous hunters he encountered.

Shooting poplar bears to relieve the boredom

During this time Lopez describes being with a team of research biologist when they dart a female polar bear for research to collect data and measurements for their fieldwork. However, when the team roll the bear over to reveal traces of menstrual blood on her white fur, he finds he is uncomfortable with the image of the bear's exposed vulnerability and has to move away while the scientists carry on with their measurements. In the course of his research on the arctic, Lopez discovered an account of how nineteenth century Whalers, having spent months trapped in the ice on their ships in the arctic, attracted polar bears by burning whale blubber so they could shoot them. One whaler recorded shooting thirty-five polar bears for sport on one afternoon and leaving the bodies on the ice. The relationship between the bears and indigenous Inuit polar bear hunters, however, is very different. In their stories the Inuit believe that animals are personified with specific intrinsic qualities; they say that polar bears can slip out of the material world and fly to the non-material spirit world.

While polar bears were hunted by the Inuit as an important source of food and fur for the whole community, they were also considered to be powerful spirit guides for shamans, when they entered the spirit world through states of self-induced trance. The shamans believed that during these trance states they travelled outside of their bodies and journeyed to the spirit world, where they could walk on the bottom of the sea. On these journeys they believed they were guided and supported by the spirit polar bears. The Inuit call the polar bear *Tôrnârssuk* "*the one who gives power*" and these flying spirit bears are depicted in the Inuit art of the Dorset culture from about 500 BC to 1000AD (Lopez, 1986).

In contrast to the "the witless insensitivity" of nineteenth century explorers, the killing of a polar bear by Inuit hunters "occurred in an atmosphere of respect with implicit spiritual obligations" (Lopez, 1986, p. 113), which involved the offering of gifts to the dead bear. These two human cultures have arrived at radically different perspectives of the relationships between humans and nature. One culture is referencing historic human social systems and the other more closely referencing a tradition of learning from the raw exposure to nature. The indigenous perspective as documented by Lopez, appears to be deeply concerned with the importance of the *relationship* between humans and animals. Death was considered a negotiable transition for the bear, from material animal to spirit animal, and the relationship between the Inuit and the polar bear endured after the bear's death.

Given the current ecological vulnerability of polar bears, the idea of nineteenth-century whalers killing polar bears for sport is akin to the kind of madness that Shepard (1982) alludes to in his book, *Nature and Madness*.

The hunters that Lopez speaks of, who have lost all sense of empathy or feeling for the animals that they killed, echoes ". . .Rene Descartes's insistence that animals feel no pain ... " (Shepard, 1982 p. 23). This particular display of a psychopathological relationship with nature, which was characteristic of the culture of that time, and was perhaps linked to the biblical narratives in Genesis of the dominion of humans over the animals and therefore a dissociated relationship with nature.

WEIRD culture still has its implicit foundation built on a platform of mechanistic science that includes linear thinking and perpetuates a disconnection with our relationship with nature, which is clearly pathologically destructive. The depth of systemic cultural change that is required to undermine these foundations is almost as unthinkable as undoing the whole industrial revolution; an overwhelming task that is often too emotionally challenging to even think about.

The limits of linear thinking

Much of contemporary biological thinking is therefore still trapped in a modernist Newtonian worldview, a viewpoint determined by mechanistic science and linear thinking and concepts. This is science that is based on the classical approach of the gathering of information, data and facts, categorization and taxonomy. It is carried out within a paradigm where consciousness and the material world are believed to be entirely separate and human and biological success is measured purely by the ability to survive. What makes this particular approach to problems so seductive is that it works really well, though only in the short term. Viewed from the perspective of a single human's lifetime, such linear thinking can make life easier or better. However, the problems only become clear when the longer ecological view, or a systemic overview, is taken into account.

For example, the development of non-biodegradable single use plastic packaging is a linear solution to the trivial problem of carrying and storing purchases. Plastic packaging is created and used for only a tiny fraction of geological or ecological time. These non-biodegradable plastics are then discarded and end up in landfill or in great plastic floating rafts in the oceans. While they can be removed from human culture, it is difficult to remove them from the ecosystem. Through the lens of systems theory we could perhaps consider plastic as the material manifestation of a philosophy that can never be challenged, a kind of material embodiment of fundamentalist linear thinking.

If plastic was the only ecological environmental pollutant, this would be enough to signal a seriously dangerous departure from thinking clearly about the safety of our environment and culture. But as we are all well aware, this is not the only case and destructive linear thinking runs through our whole culture, from production and consumption to waste management. Linear thinking continues through the seeking of solutions to these problems. Even though we are encouraged to recycle non-biodegradable plastics into other non-biodegradable products, we are simply moving the problem slightly further down the timeline, without producing any fundamental systemic change.

Mechanomorphism; seeing nature as a machine

The type of thinking that works for mechanical systems therefore does not work for living systems that, unlike machines, have the capacity to sense their inner and outer environment, evaluate, respond, and change. As Gregory Bateson observes, nature functions at a level of organization that cannot be described in logical terms. In fact he tells us that, "Logic and quantity turnout to be in appropriate devices for describing organisms and their interactions and internal organization" (Bateson, 1997, p. 20).

Yet what we know about nature, including ourselves, is that we are complex combinations of natural systems that have managed to self-regulate, reproduce, evolve, grow, and make unpredictable responses to environmental change. The idea that nature works like a machine, like a car or a computer, is a type of "mecanomorphism", in which we avoid looking at complexity and use recent simple ideas to try to understand very old and very complex problems (Buhner, 2014, p. 110).

This mechanistic view of biology therefore has some serious limitations. It has not halted the progressive destruction of the planet's ecosystems, nor does it allow for the emergence of any new possible narratives or thinking. What this approach does is unconsciously reinforce the idea that we have one system operating in nature and quite another in human systems. Though the implicit subtlety of this split in the relationship between humans and the rest of nature is discussed within the context of ecopsychology, it does not get into the biology textbooks. It is as if the natural sciences have been telling us that humans live in a separate world from the rest of nature; humans in the perceived sustainable ecology of our living rooms, and polar bears in the unsustainable ecology of the arctic. And of course the link between the two is invisible and usually not explicit. Although the language of contemporary biology and ecology has created a world that can be scientifically explained, it leaves the human population in exile from the rest of nature and we are stuck in a self-referencing mechanistic narrative with no way out.

Attachment patterns and nature

To find a way out of this dilemma it is helpful to explore the current research and understanding of both attachment and systems theory and how trauma is implicated in both of these concepts. Developmental trauma is now being understood to be a major underlying root of many of our current mental health and social difficulties (Van de Kolk, 2014). The effects of trauma can lead to a condition where we do not have the words to describe our own feelings and are unable able to feel or recognize our own emotions and as a result are not able to understand what others might be feeling. This loss of the ability to recognize feelings, which can happen early in life as a result of abuse or loss of a sense of belonging, can result in a reduced ability to understand subtle relational interactions with the world. In this state we can no longer make sense or understand clearly the signs we are receiving from others and this can seriously limit our capacity for self-reflection on how we relate to others (Van de Kolk, 2014).

Crittenden (2008), a developmental psychopathologist who studied attachment, describes what happens to children who have suffered loss. Essentially, she says that they are unable to accurately read the signs and signals from the world and this can be potentially dangerous because they are unable to change their behavioural responses. Crittenden believes these fixed behaviours and worldviews are driven by unconscious preverbal implicit memory patterns that she calls "dispositional representations" that become maladaptive attachment systems or patterns that restrict the accuracy of our thoughts and feelings (Crittenden, 2008, p. 92). There are two types of maladaptations that she identifies: an *Avoidant Attachment Style*, where *thinking* is used to organize how we see the world and feelings are considered inaccurate or not felt at all, and an *Anxious Ambivalent Attachment Style*, where *feelings* are used to engage in the relational world and thinking is considered inaccurate or absent. However, both conditions prevent an accurate reading of relationships that people have with each other (Crittenden & Landini, 2015, p. 111).

Hence the value of psychotherapy is that it can help us to recognize where our thoughts, feelings, and behaviours are predetermined by our old stories and our unconscious but implicit memory patterns. And in recognizing this, it is possible to begin to learn to see the world differently. Without the insight of a reflective practice such as psychotherapy, these maladaptive patterns remain unchallenged in our memory systems, and as such become default ways of seeing the world.

Biologists, from Charles Darwin to Richard Dawkins, have accumulated facts to explain the complexity of nature, and we can now understand these relationships, in terms of energy, survival mechanisms, and genetics. However, this certainty is less valuable for having an understanding of the systems of intimate emotional relationships. For instance, the subtlety of the relationship between the Inuit hunters and the polar bears, show how difficult it can be to value relationships that we do not really understand.

Our current mechanistic biological thinking has some of its roots in the ideas and work of Rene Descartes and Charles Darwin, both men developed their ideas before the development of psychotherapeutic thinking, and both men suffered early maternal loss. It is possible that this biographical experience has a potentially significant influence on how we think, see, and engage with the world. Descartes' mother died when he was only a two and his father encouraged him into a highly intellectual education from a young age. It is also worth remembering that Descartes dissected living dogs in order to study their circulation, and describes his experience of putting his finger inside the heart of a live dog and feeling the pulse of the heart muscle (Sheldrake, 2012). In the light of current psychotherapy and attachment theory, we might understand Descartes' extreme lack of empathy or interest in a relationship with animals as a form of psychopathology or maladaptive attachment pattern.

Darwin's mother also died when he was a child and his father and older sisters told him he should never speak of her again. He did this so thoroughly that as an adult, while playing a word game with his children, he argued that there was no such word as *M.O.T.H.E.R.* It is therefore possible that this loss could have influenced Darwin's belief in the primacy of survival. This is a belief characteristic of an avoidant attachment pattern, in which an experience of terrifying relational uncertainly makes personal survival a safer focus than the feelings of the loss of love and relationship.

Learning to think systemically by observing nature

An alternative to the practice of using a mechanistic approach to encountering the world involves developing the skill of systemic thinking. This involves a somewhat slow process of unlearning the habit of intellectual thinking, which is deeply embedded in WEIRD culture. While we are very familiar with the habit of learning to think logically and linearly, we are unlikely to come across systemic thinking in school and it is usually only learnt as part of a more specialist education.

Systems thinking that is used in the practice of systemic family therapy attempts to avoid linearity and focuses on relationships by attempting to pay attention in a way that is respectful, non-hierarchal, emergent, hopeful, and open to the possibility of systemic change. This stance makes space for the recognition that complex human and natural systems can never be fully known or explained in concepts or linear logic. This promotes openness to "not knowing" and the possibility of exploring multiple perspectives, rather than attempting to capture the understanding of a situation in a single truth.

The practice of systemic family therapy grew out of the study of cybernetics, and Bateson's ideas about nature and the study of self-regulatory systems, their constraints and their possibilities. Systems, including natural ecosystems and human systems, are characterized by a quality of *wholeness* and therefore cannot be understood by being broken down into smaller parts. Wholeness cannot be discovered by dissection of a system; since it is *non-summative*, it is more than the sum of its parts.

In nature we see climax ecosystems of old growth forests as complex examples of wholeness. Although made up of many tree and plant species, a healthy ecosystem as such cannot be recreated simply by planting new trees. The quality of wholeness in systems is not an object or a bigger component part, but a pattern that is in constant movement around a set of qualities and exists in *dynamic equilibrium*, maintaining its stability through the process of *homeostasis.* This quality of wholeness also has the characteristic of being holographic. This means that the dynamic equilibrium can be maintained even if the size of the system is increased or reduced, and the stability of a system can be achieved and arrive at homoeostasis from any number of different pathways, a quality called *equifinality.* Again we see this in forest ecosystems where natural or human destruction triggers the forest to regenerate back to a climax ecosystem, although the way it does this would be different in every situation.

Complex systems therefore have an inherent ability to recognize information and to communicate and respond accordingly and this can be seen in ecosystems, human family systems, as well as within organizations. This means that systems have the capacity to constantly monitor internal and external changes and to respond to feedback so that its own continuity is ensured (Jones, 1993).

Biological systems can also respond to internal and external environmental pressure by going through the process of complete and catastrophic reorganization or metamorphosis and the re-establishing of dynamic stability at another level, a process also known as *phase change* (Suchantke, 2009). We can see this in the way that plants change systemically, as they move from a leafing stage to the flowing stage, and also from the flowering stage to the fruiting stage, each stage moving into the next, characterized by specific biochemistry, processes, and form.

The herbalist, poet, and systems thinker Stephen Harrod Buhner combining ideas from Gregory Bateson, Chaos theory, and Systems theory, uses the metaphor of a street juggler to provide a picture of how nature's complex non-linear systems work (Buhner, 2014, p. 74). The skill of learning to juggle comes from long practice and is an example of a state of dynamic equilibrium, where tiny interacting processes keeps the balls in the air, involving adjustments that are too complex to be analysed or documented using linear thinking. Juggling cannot be learnt through an intellectual process, but has to be learnt as tacit knowledge, through "feel" or "sensing into" the constantly and minutely adjusted, self-organizing system of interactions between the moving balls, hands, and feet, in order to maintain a balance point.

Juggling is just one example of what systems theorists call *emergent behaviour*; a complex pattern of stability that emerges spontaneously from dynamic systems. Two jugglers starting at the same time and place could never move predictably in the same way, as each is constantly responding to the dynamic interface between the internal and external information to reach a point of equifinality, thus keeping the balls in the air. The interactions between the movement of the balls and the surface of the floor, muscle tone, body posture, and balance, are all processed in the body below conscience awareness.

A skilled juggler is able to play with the edges of a stable system by moving about, passing a ball under her leg, singing a song, or interacting with the audience, and yet still maintain and enjoy the dynamic equilibrium. This is similar to how complex ecosystems maintain equilibrium, and like the juggler they are able to respond to external and internal changes to create emergent processes while still maintaining a systemic balance. This is only the case up to a point, because beyond a certain stage the system will collapse catastrophically and the juggler will drop the balls. An example of this rapid catastrophic change in a system, or *phase change*, is the cooling of water. Water remains liquid down to zero degrees Celsius, and then undergoes a rapid phase change and becomes ice; in most complex systems the precise point where catastrophic breakdown occurs cannot be predicted. If we are stuck in thinking linearly we might not be able to sense or feel, like a juggler, that the system is moving towards phase change until it is too late.

When we observe systems in nature it becomes clear that they are not uniformly patterned and some points in a system include nodes of more concentrated information, which can have the capacity to trigger systemic transformation or phase change. Although systems can remain very stable in the face of internal and external input, Bateson recognized systemic change can be triggered by input to specific points of instability or by reaching a particular threshold of complexity.

We can see this manifest in the study of botany and plant growth where most plant tissue cells can expand and only grow in size, elongating the structure of leaves and stems. However in specific places, such as the growing tips and the cambium, there are cells called *plant meristems* that have the capacity to divide and make new and different type of tissue cells; meristems are the nodes that make the difference in plant growth. One example of this are the nodes or eyes in potatoes, that have the capacity to grow into new potato pants. In fungi, spores are more sophisticated nodes and have the same capacity to make a difference vegetatively and are moved passively by water and wind. In flowering plants, seeds perform a similar function, but have the added difference of carrying new combinations of genetic material, so have a greater capacity to make a more complex difference.

In animals, unlike plants almost all cells can divide to make new tissues, all animal cells are the equivalent of *plant meristems*, so in a sense, animals are a collection of organized meristems and have the even greater capacity to bring about change in their environment than plants through their ability of conscious movement. Using this way of thinking humans can be seen as self-conscious meristems; nodes of complex information with the capacity to make a conscious difference to their environment. The quality of this difference is determined by our awareness and capacity to process complex information.

This type of systems thinking, based on studies of how nature works, can lead to the recognition that there are not really any linear systems in nature, they only appear to be linear if they are observed within a very narrow context. If we widen the context using a meta outlook, what appears to be stable or sustainable, from a systemic perspective, is actually in constant dynamic equilibrium, always changing and readjusting itself, and open to the possibility of catastrophic or creative transformation.

Challenges to the modernism of contemporary biology are surprisingly uncommon with a few exceptions such as the work of Elisabet Sahtouris (2000) who describes a more systemic or neo-indigenous story of evolution, and John Launer who points out the paradox of the widening gap between biological and psychological thinking (Launer, 2001). If ecosystems are in essence communication systems, then they must be communicating in a language that is accessible to all parts of the ecosystem and this language might be easy to read, if we know how to look for it. But in order to read nature's language, her open secret, we have to give up the cultural habit of using an intellectual analysis of the world, a potentially difficult and emotionally painful process.

To understand the natural world as a system Mary Catherine Bateson suggests we have to let go of the idea of nature being made up of concepts or interchangeable parts, like a children's toy farm or zoo. The idea that the environment is a place, like a stage on which humans and animals play out their lives, is a product of unhelpful linear, Newtonian, mechanical thinking. Mary Bateson suggests, we need to learn a new language, and

> If we want to talk about the living world and ourselves we need to master the disciplines of descriptions and references in this curious language that has no things in it but only differences and relationships.
>
> (Bateson & Bateson, 2005, p. 191)

In a similar vein, biologist Richard Lewontin (2001) has applied systems thinking to his observation of ecosystems and comes to the conclusion that the boundary or distinction between species and their environment is an artificial separation, a legacy of mechanistic thinking that is looking for the separate building blocks of nature. He believes that when thinking about nature from a systemic perspective, organisms cannot be usefully thought about as separated from their environment, because the systemic interaction between the evolution of species and their environment is so tightly coupled that organism and environment are two different manifestations of the same system. He explains that

> The properties of species map the shape of the underlying external world, just as when we sprinkle iron filings on a sheet of paper lying over a magnet, the

filings form a pattern that maps the underlying magnetic field. In a curious sense the study of organisms is really a study of the shape of the environmental space, the organisms themselves being nothing but the passive medium through which we see the shape of the external world. They are the iron filings of the environmental field.

(Lewontin, 2001, p. 44)

Buhner comes to similar conclusion and describes this view as where

. . .there can be no definite boundary line between environment and organism, for there is *only* environment. What we really are dealing with in this scenario that we call the world is an uncountable complexity of nested and overlapping self-organized systems, each of them an aspect.

(Buhner, 2014, p. 238)

If we think about nature from a systemic perspective we have to let go of all the ideas of concepts and things; we cannot conceptually separate organisms from their environment. Instead, we have to think of the whole of nature as a matrix of complex fractal patterns that presents itself as raw sensory experience. Biologist Jesper Hoffmeyer (2008) describes how we are living in a sphere of dynamic patterns of sensory communications and signals; not an environment but a *semiosphere*. He explains this by saying that we are surrounded by a sphere of sensory patterns that do not contain any intrinsic concepts. We can begin to make sense of this matrix in nature through the non-conceptual hermeneutic practice of reading signs, known as semiotics, a process that Pat Crittenden (2015) also recommends to help read the complex implicit patterns of our attachment behaviours and how we relate others.

From this perspective nature is not made up of interactive component parts that we can control, but is more like complex patterns of interacting messages. Seen in this way animal and plant forms – whether as leaf, flowers, bones, organs, individual species – are particular concentrations of these messages manifested in a physical form. They are the nodes embedded within networks of a systemic matrix that reveal some of the archetypal patterns of the whole system; they are messages written in nature's creatural language. Hoffmeyer further tells us that these systemic patterns that we experience in the semiosphere are not just a passive background activity but are in fact *communicative systems*; they are *somebodies* (Hoffmeyer, 2008). This way of seeing the imaginal patterning of nature, requiring the semiotic skill of pattern reading, has been described in detail by a broad range of original thinkers, specifically: Henry Bortoft (1996), Gregory and Mary Bateson (1979, 2005), Henry Corbin (Cheetham, 2003, 2015), Robert Romanyshyn (1999, 2007), Rudolf Steiner (2000), and Stephen Buhner (2014).

The process of acquiring a hermeneutic practice is a very slow skill to learn and can take many years to master and is particularly difficult for those who have had a formal reductionist scientific education. Reading nature's creatural/imaginal language is a feeling process that needs a clear and unrestricted relationship with the subtlety of personal feelings. This means that the challenge of understanding nature in this way begins to cross over from just an ecological understanding of nature to a psychotherapeutic understanding of oneself. We cannot think systemically unless we can be self-reflective about how our implicit emotions organize our thoughts. Nor can we if we are restricted to conceptual or siloed thinking because systemic thinking is transgressive; it does not recognize or respect the limitations of socially or personally constructed barriers. This way of engaging with natural phenomena that is non-conceptual, slow, and embodied, can lead to a personal and transformational way of engaging with world (Romanyshyn, 2007, p. 233).

To experience the natural world in this way we need to peel away our current stories about nature and let go of biological modernism, intellectual expertise, and ideas about the role of survival mechanisms as the only agent for the evolution of form and process. In WEIRD culture these views are usually adhesively attached to our perceptions and to let go of them requires considerable effort and self-reflection. But if we do manage to let go of these ideas, we are left with the freedom to look at the patterns in the semiosphere that surrounds us in the other-than-human world, as well as within our internal psychological world. We can begin to have the unsettling experience of recognizing that the organizing patterns and relationship systems in both nature and psyche are *somebodies* with which we can communicate through process of intersubjective ecopsychotherapy.

The Sentience of nature

Bacterial geneticist James Shapiro describes how bacteria, considered to be the simplest and oldest organisms, are now being recognized as having the characteristics of sentient life forms. He says:

> Bacteria utilize sophisticated mechanisms for intercellular communication and even have the ability to commandeer the basic cell biology of higher plants and animals to meet their own basic needs. This remarkable series of observations require us to revise basic ideas about biological information processing and recognize that even the smallest cells are sentient beings.
>
> (Buhner, 2014, p. 103)

Bacteria that have negotiated the catastrophic environmental changes in the atmosphere, from anaerobic to oxygen rich during the early evolution of life on earth, during one human lifespan, have developed the capacity to become resistance to a wide spectrum of antibiotics. This has the potential of undermining the foundations of *modern medicine* that was built on the mistaken belief that it's possible to kill off one part of an ecosystem without any other systemic impact.

The idea that nature itself is sentient, and talking to us, is also something that indigenous people have been telling WEIRD culture for a long time but it is very difficult to hear when we are convinced of our mechanistic human centric perspective. It is alleged that Chief Luther Standing Bear said that,

> Kinship with all creatures of the earth, sky, and water was a real and active principle. For the animal and bird world there existed a brotherly feeling that kept the Lakota safe among them. And so close did some of the Lakotas come to their feathered and furred friends that in true brotherhood they spoke a common tongue.
>
> (McLuhan, 1971, p. 6)

Likewise, McLuhan tells us that Tatanga Mani said,

> Do you know that trees talk? Well they do. They talk to each other, and they'll talk to you, if you listen. The trouble is, white people didn't listen. They never listened to the Indians, so I don't suppose they'll listen to the other voices in nature.
>
> (McLuhan, 1971, p. 23)

It seems possible that the process of transference and countertransference experienced in therapy, does not only occur between humans, but extends far into the more than human relationships to "all our relations": the plants, animals, and even the earth itself. Bateson's exploration for *"patterns that connect"* is not an intellectual pursuit, but the hunt for patterns that we can connect with, aesthetically or emotionally. He suggests that if we connect with these emotions we might be able to join in this conversation with nature and understand what the earth is telling us (Bateson, 1979, p. 9).

While living systems do not communicate using quantification or measurement, they are able to respond to subtleties in qualitative phenomena, often missed in evidence-based research such as "contrast, frequency, symmetry, correspondence, relation, and congruence and conformity" (Hoffmeyer, 2008, p. 29). Whereas the creatural and imaginal do not reflect factual information that can be proved, they do provide a level of knowing. This is an emergence and intersubjective experience that occurs within the relationship between two *somebodies* and as such is not true in the factual sense of cause and effect, but true in the way love is true, and is learnt through the way of the heart (Cheetham, 2015, p. 137).

The slow and personal process of building a new relationship with nature began for me with my encounter with the skull of the mouse. Over the years, it involved the difficult and challenging process of unlearning what most of us assume to be true, and learning instead to trust what I experienced as being important. It is possible to read imaginal language in the form of messages that we recognize in the shape of plants and animals, as well as biological processes and metamorphoses. There is useful imaginal scaffolding to be found in these biological processes such as: mitosis, meiosis, seed formation, dormancy, germination, leafing, flowering, fertilization, seed dispersal, and fruiting which can be used to describe natural as well as psychological phenomenon,. These processes can also be thought of as nodes or *keystone patterns* that are found in nature. Though their complexity is not fully described by concepts and are better captured in alchemical language of the imaginal and the language of systemic processes, which can reveal implicit underlying pattern structures in the semiosphere.

Patterns in plant and animal form

Having been trained as a biologist that all forms and patterns in nature were a result of random genetic mutations and blind natural selection, I did not expect to encounter any intrinsic order in nature. However as a young biology teacher, preparing lessons in a Rudolf Steiner school, I was surprised to come across the persistent and reoccurring imaginal or creatural patterns in biology, as indicated by Steiner and those who have followed his work (Schad, 1977).

I was already familiar with the three germ layers in embryology, the primitive polarity between the ectoderm; from which the nervous system develops and the endoderm that gives rise to the digestive system. I also knew how a third more complex layer, the mesoderm, arises between the two that becomes the origin of the heart and circulatory system in higher animals. But based on the work of Wolfgang Schad, Andreas Suchantke (2009) shows how this motif in the germ layers can be seen as a type of *keystone pattern* in the organization of biological systems. He shows how the three largest mammals groups, the ungulates, carnivores, and rodents, each have a particular development of one of these three characteristics: digestion system, sensory nervous system, and circulatory system. The ungulates, the hooved and long-legged grazing animals of open grassland, have a specialization in their digestion for low energy plant foods and the development of rumination with the aid of microorganism. In contrast the rodents are short-legged creatures that have a tendency to live in burrows, feed on high-energy foods such as grain and seed, and have a highly developed nervous system for both sight and hearing.

The populations of these two mammal groups are moderated by the activities of the carnivores, which predate on both groups and hold a position of balance in the ecosystems. Suchantke also illustrates how these patterns can be seen in the teeth of the groups, ungulate's skulls have well developed sets of molars at the back of the mouth and reduced or absent incisors, in contrast rodents have well-developed incisors in the front and reduced molars, neither the ungulates or rodent have very well developed canines. However, carnivores have well developed canine teeth that sit between the incisors and molars, whereas in ungulates and rodents they just have a gap in the middle position known as the daistema (Suchantke, 2009, p. 136).

By observing patterns in nature without concepts and the idea of functionality, biologist Wolfgang Schad recognizes this *keystone patterning* that is repeated in the human skeleton. He contrasts the rounded enclosing skull with concentration of sense organs, with the digestive quality of the lower body and the long limb bones (Schad, 1977). Like the patterns in the rodents and ungulates, the thorax, with its combination of both motifs, mediates this polarity. This triune pattern is repeated in the individual limb bones; for example, the femur has a *head* at the upper end, a bifurcation into the condyles of the knee joint at the other, and a subtle twist in between. This pattern of bifurcation starting at the condyles of the femur continues along the limb into the tibia and fibula and again into the bones of the feet, the tarsals, metatarsals, and phalanges. The same pattern can be seen in the skeleton of the arm, with the humerus, radius, ulna, and carpels.

This triune pattern is also repeated in plants. Where in humans the rounded skull and the heads of the bones are orientated upwards from a geocentric perspective, this rounded shape in plants is found in the root sphere. Both Rudolf Steiner and Charles Darwin identified head or nerve like qualities in the activities of the roots that sense their environment and determine activities of the upper plant. Darwin tells us that

> . . .it is hardly an exaggeration to say that the tip of the radicle thus endowed [with sensitivity] and having the power of directing the movement of the adjoining parts acts like the brain of one of the lower animals . . . receiving impressions from sense–organs and directing the several movements.
>
> (Buhner, 2014, p. 111)

But plant and animal form manifest opposite gestures. While the elongated and bifurcating limbs of animals orientate downwards, the forked branching of tree and plant stems orientated upwards. And the delicacy of the leaves in this pattern mirrors the fingers and toes. This observation leads to startling images of plants being orientated in the polar opposite way to humans, with their brain-like roots in the ground and with their bifurcating branches and shoots growing up like limbs.

With plants, these polarities of the head and limb gesture are mediated or crossover at the surface of the ground. We also see this in the strange cross over of the vascular tissue at this point, which reorientates from the centre of the root to the periphery in the stem. However, the formation of flowers shows a different order of patterning, a phase change or metamorphosis from the photosynthetic and autotrophic leaf to the non-photosynthetic and heterotopic flower. The process of pollination and fertilization in flowering plants, showing the imaginal pattern of death, transformation, and rebirth, is remarkably similar to the psychological transition of adolescent rites of passage.

Patterns in process

In a similar way to tracking animal prints through the forest, we can follow patterns not only in form but also in biologic processes. One example is the *phase change* or *metamorphosis* from the asexual to the sexual stage in butterflies that occurs during pupation and the formation of the chrysalis. The caterpillar, the asexual stage of grow, gradually slows down prior to pupation and forms a cocoon in which the caterpillar's body completely dissolves itself and the new reproductive butterfly grows from a few simple cells within the chrysalis. By following this process without concepts, but aesthetically, we can observe the same isomorphic shape or pattern, in the formation of flowers in plants. As the plant grows towards flowering, the non-reproductive process of the leaf reduces in size and complexity and the leaf stem undergoes a *metamorphosis* into the petals of the flower (Suchantke, 2009, p. 62). The leaf and the caterpillar both undergo a complete reduction in these change processes, almost a death process, in order to give rise to the new reproductive forms of the flower and the butterfly respectively. The emergent forms of the flower and the butterflies then become two complimentary but separate parts of the more complex relationship systems of pollination and fertilization in the sexual reproduction of plants.

Reading the *creatural grammar* of *phase change* that manifests in biology, such as pupation and the flowering of plants, may provide insight into the isomorphic processes of adolescent development and could usefully inform some aspect of psychotherapeutic understanding (Bateson & Bateson, 2005, p. 192). As such, these observations do not deny the established evidence for evolution but these patterns do appear to be operating independently of what we understand as evolutionary mechanisms; they seem to be manifestations of some underlying organization in the wholeness of biological systems. Like the Inuit spirit polar bear, these patterns are *transgressive*, and do not recognize social constructed borders of human ideas, concepts, or boundaries within systems. They can move from system to system through nested hierarchies, from the cellular level to the ecological level, to the psychological level, and everywhere in between.

Since our relationship to nature is strongly influenced by social context, what was considered to be acceptable to nineteenth century Whalers might be considered a type of madness today. Our great grandchildren will more than likely look back on our use of fossil fuels and the ecological destruction that underpins our culture in a different way than we do. When we think about our current understanding of nature from a systemic perspective it seems unlikely that human concepts, a relatively recent development in the earth's history, are inadequate to fully describe the complexity of natural ecosystems that predate human thinking by many hundreds of millennia. If this is the case it seems entirely possible that how nature works is not completely captured by the approach and language of biological science.

While nature does appear capable of communicating with itself through signs, signals, and patterns in a sophisticated and complex systemic language that ensures change and stability, it's not clear that human thinking is fully able to read these communication systems. Our current understanding of nature, based on linear thinking and a pleromal understanding of the physical mechanisms at work, has not been completely successful in preventing environmental destruction or the degradation of human psychological health. Learning to read the creatural or imaginal language of nature can compliment the limitations of pleromal thinking and reveal new information about how nature and the human mind work. Perhaps this way of reading nature has the potential to open a door to a different quality of thinking about biology and could reveal more ecologically stable ways of living on the earth.

Using pleromal thinking to understand nature we see only the physical mechanisms and this leads to the illusion that we can control nature as if it were a machine, perpetuating the WEIRD belief that human systems and the ecosystem can function separately from each other. This approach can overlook the fact that nature is a sensitive, emergent, and interactive balance that is constantly dancing at the edge of systemic change and every human action influences the whole. By using creatural and imaginal thinking there is an opportunity for a more subtle observation of nature's complex relationships and patterns that can gradually change human thinking to be more attuned to how nature works. And this opportunity should be the birthright of future generations.

Chapter 8

Reimagining human development

In his book, *Wild Therapy*, body based psychotherapist Nick Totton (2011) provides many examples of the raw and ragged edges in the relationship between domesticated and wild nature. He outlines the inadequacy of current conceptual models and the destruction this has brought, through the devastation of the natural environment and the wild aspects of human nature, including the legacy of imperial conquest and control of indigenous peoples. Totton believes that although wild therapy has many approaches to the work, he suggests it is an "attitude of mind" rather than a set of particular techniques (Totton, 2011, p. 181). What he describes is an attitude of mind that recognizes that wild therapy is a healing practice that is essentially relational, emergent, embodied, and spontaneous.

Rewilding psychotherapy and education

Totton describes how ecotherapists have made the move out of the indoor clinical setting to practice therapy in nature. However, this change of attitude could also include allowing the wild and other-than-human to enter the clinic room during therapy, as images or dreams, animals, plants, and natural materials. While this perspective on ecopsychotherapy includes a combination of specific techniques and direct engagement with nature, it also requires a radical change of attitude away from the current WEIRD worldview to an ecopsychological or more indigenous worldview of mental health and human development.

The late Martin Jordan provided a very clear overview of the range of nature based therapy techniques. However, he also acknowledged that the field of ecopsychology and ecotherapy sometimes lacks a coherent link to mainstream approaches, as well as a comprehensive model of how to practice therapy in outdoor natural spaces (Jordan, 2015). Despite excellent work in this field, the practice is highly diverse and does not have professional recognition or regulation. Nature based therapy seems to have emerged spontaneously from a variety of different directions and fields of practice, such as deep ecology, outdoor and experiential education, horticultural therapy, and therapeutic work with animals. And although described as therapeutic they are not clearly contained within mainstream counselling and psychotherapy practices. Jordan gathered examples from a wide range of work that includes adventure therapy, ecotherapy, wilderness therapy, nature therapy, nature guided therapy, as well as vision fast and soul craft work.

Beyond the borders of mental health formulation

Current therapy practice is, perhaps rightly, highly regulated and benchmarked against scientific paradigms. Therefore, only evidence based practice is considered to be effective and new emergent practices are judged against the medical model and scientific criteria. Some years ago I gave a talk on ecotherapy to a group of medical professionals, made up of psychiatrists and psychologists. They listened to what I had to say and really appreciated the value of this approach but at the end someone said that although this made a lot of sense to them, they thought that if they asked their manager about using some of these approaches they would say that it was all just "hippy shit".

Recent developments in the practice and use of mindfulness in mental health is a good example of how a practice that was once considered just "hippy shit' has crossed over into mainstream practice, supported by a strong evidence base for its effectiveness. We do not need to look very deeply into current WEIRD mental health models to discover an implicit and sometimes explicit paradigm of mental health care that is based on the medical model. This way of thinking views mental health with the same lens as physical health conditions, in which mental health is considered to be a disease or disorder, produced by a hidden cause or agent, which once identified, can be successfully cured with the correct treatment by expert clinicians. Consultant Clinical Psychologist Professor Peter Kinderman of University of Liverpool, and his colleagues, have challenged this idea of a diagnostic approach and highlights this when they say they have ". . .identified serious inadequacies in the specific proposed revisions, and has also highlighted scientific, philosophical, practical and humanitarian weaknesses in the diagnostic approach to psychological well-being, underpinning the DSM" (Kinderman, Read, Moncrieff, & Bentall, 2012, p. 2).

What Kinderman and his colleagues are referring to is the American Psychiatric Association's *Diagnostic and Statistical Manual* (the DSM) (APA, 1952), a reference that defines psychological distress in the language of biological illness. For example autonomic biological human responses to the trauma of war or terrible loss are categorized in the DSM as Post-traumatic Stress Disorder (PTSD). Ethical and philosophical issues with the medical model of mental health are not new. Avoiding treating such mental health issues as a biological illness was part of the original impulse by the Milan Group of Family Therapists, in order to develop a more systemic approach to treating mental health; these perspectives have now been widely incorporated into systemic therapeutic practice.

Towards a systemic ecopsychological mental health formulation

Widening this medical view to include an ecopsychological perspective, we see that despite the huge changes in our human made environment of the last

10,000 years, the current physical and psychological make up of humans is essentially the same as our indigenous hunter-gatherer ancestors. Although it is possible for polar bears to survive, and perhaps even breed in captivity in a temperate city zoo, it is difficult to escape the fact that this is not their natural environment and they are merely and perhaps barely surviving outside of their particular environmental context. Like the polar bears in the San Diego Zoo, humans in WEIRD culture are surviving outside their natural habitat. One of the major difference between indigenous hunter-gatherers and ourselves, is that we have lost or altered a lot of our natural environmental context.

Where we have mostly lost our tribal and filial groups and extended family support, in WIERD culture it has been replaced with a socially constructed context of the media, or other social, political, and religious groups and work place culture. For many people in Western culture we have mostly lost free access to the land and the opportunity to spend all of our days moving through the landscape. We have lost daily close contact and observation of animals and plants and the somatic and sensory experiences of the life and death processes in nature. And we have mostly lost our knowledge and stories of our ancestors and elders, as well as our awareness of a nature based spirituality that included socially sanctioned nature based community rituals and celebrations. This is not a new idea, given that Bateson believed we have lost "the sense of parallelism between man's organization and that of the animals and plants" (Bateson, 1979, p. 18). We have lost a deep sense of belonging or as Tom Cheetham suggests, "The soul is in exile in the modern world — there is no place for it in the world of historical, material causality" (Cheetham, 2003, p. 64).

These experiences of nature, that our hunter-gatherer ancestors encountered every day, might appear to be no longer relevant within developed Western culture. Nevertheless, it seems very likely that they are highly valuable and developmentally important for the healthy physiological and psychological growth of our ancient hunter-gatherer psyches and bodies. It is also likely that the deep and unacknowledged grief of this loss still drives some of the unconscious and destructive aspects of WEIRD cultural behaviour, and will continue to do so until it is socially and psychologically integrated (Shepard, 1982). The American First Nation's Lakota Chief, Luther Standing Bear, recognized the significant consequences of this loss within his culture when he said,

> The old Lakota was wise. He knew that man's heart away from nature becomes hard; he knew that lack of respect for growing, living things soon led to a lack of respect for humans too. So he kept his youth close to its softening influence.
>
> (McLuhan, 1971, p. 6)

From an ecopsychology perspective it is acknowledged that we are all still recovering refugees from a hunter-gatherer lifestyle. This experience, and possibly the trans-generational trauma of this change, has shaped our developmental needs and human cultures since the time of the Pleistocene (Glendenning, 1994; Shepard, 1998). Though this idea that WEIRD culture has lost something important during the process of civilization may seem challenging or unrealistic within most current mental health and education settings, it is a potentially useful imaginal picture of an important and deeply *subjugated narrative*; a lost story (White & Epston, 1990; Glendenning, 1994). In fact this way of thinking could provide a starting point for the formulation of interventions to support the most troubled young people in our culture, and rethink their development. Thus an ecopsychology perspective could also contribute to defining a pathway to psychological and cultural renewal by reconnecting the split between contemporary psychological and ecological perspectives.

Malidoma Somé (1995), in his book on traditional initiation practices in the West African Dagara tribe, writes about his own tribal initiation on returning to his village after fifteen years of being forcibly removed to live in a Jesuit boarding school. In Dagara culture children were believed to have contact with the spirit world prior to their birth and to arrive with a purpose, which they gradually forget. And their elders where revered for being close to death and the threshold of the spirit world, from where the children had just arrived. Somé describes the cultural significance of initiatory rites of passage in Dagara culture as a way that adolescents were supported to remember their own unique purpose during the process of their adolescent initiation, as well as the healing gift they might bring to their culture. This perspective turns Western paternalism on its head, so that direction of cultural change is guided not by tradition and adult decisions, but by the emergent voices and visions of the next generation.

James Hillman describes a similar formulation in his a*corn theory*, the idea that "each person bears a uniqueness that asks to be lived and this is already present before it can be lived" (Hillman, 1997, p. 6). He draws his ideas from Plato who refers to this unique aspect of each person as a pattern or image that the Greeks called the "daimon" and the Romans called our "genius" (Hillman, 1997, p. 8). A similar perspective is found in Archbishop Desmond Tutu's forward to the book *Reclaiming Youth at Risk* where he describes how we might approach working with challenging and excluded youth. He says,

> We ought to be saying, "we have a deep reverence for you, little one, because even though you may be a problem, you are a God-carrier. You belong to God". Each of Gods children has a preciousness that cannot be measured. If we don't do all we can to salvage these children, it is almost like spitting in the face of God.
>
> (Brendtro, Brokenleg, & Van Brockern, 1990, p. x)

WEIRD culture is usually more comfortable thinking about our relationships with children in a more linear way, with the idea that children's lives are directed by genes or family traits and traditions that will determine individual characters, or sometimes even more mechanistically as blank slates or empty vessels, to be filled with information in the process of adult directed education and socialization. The perspective of Hillman, Tutu, and Somé, is not usually used in contemporary therapeutic and educational thinking.

Expanding on this perspective to include an ecopsychological viewpoint, the unborn child could be imagined using Hillman's (1997) nature based metaphor of a seed, like an acorn, which contains within it an emergent pattern of potential to become a unique individual tree, rather that the mechanistic metaphor of a computer programme with predetermined circuits or neural pathways. In this formulation each child can be seen as less controlled by the past and deterministic genetics, but is invited to *grow down* into a unique expression, the quality and fullness of this expression being drawn out by life opportunities and exposure to facilitating environments (Hillman, 1997, p. 41). If we reframe our perception of the human position on the earth to include our long indigenous perspective, it becomes pretty clear that the current narrative of humanity as "consumers" or as a purely destructive evolutionary dead-end, is not only very narrow, but also leads to a limited imagination for how we might find a sustainable way forward.

Combining the clinical and the imaginal perspectives

There is an old tale from England that describes how a woman, who falls on hard times, and goes in search of work and unknowingly accepts the task of caring for the child of a fairy queen. She is instructed to care for the child with specific instructions to use a special ointment that she must rub into the baby's skin morning and night. One night the woman inadvertently rubs her own eye with her oily finger and discovers that the ointment gives her the ability to see into a previously invisible fairy realm. With one eye she sees the word of men and women and with the anointed eye she can see beyond into the magical world of the fairy folk. This story can be used as metaphor for how professionals combine mainstream and imaginal aspects of therapeutic work into an integrated ecopsychological approach.

Perhaps it is useful to approach mental health with this two-eyed perspective, with one eye on diagnosis, care plans, clinical formulation, risk assessments, and professional accountability, and the other eye on the imaginal. In clinical practice this imaginal eye would have an awareness of working with the unspoken, body based, and imaginal messages, as well as the wider ecopsychological and *soul centric* context of what is being presented.

In his book, *The Master and his Emissary*, psychiatrist Iain McGilchrist describes how the two hemispheres of the brain, just like the woman in the story, see the world in two different ways. The left-brain processes information about the world within a closed system by self-referencing and by the, "mechanical rearrangement of other things already known" (McGilchrist, 2009, p. 174). This left-brain perspective appears to be trapped in a mechanistic view and has a "dismissive attitude to anything outside of its limited focus" so that it can never know anything new (McGilchrist, 2009, p. 429). In contrast the right brain, the view through the anointed eye, is "conscious of the other" and can hold a more reflexive picture of the world as "never fully graspable" and so remains open to the emergent and not yet known (McGilchrist, 2009, p. 174).

Family therapists are used to working with seeing in two ways by using Bateson's *double description.* An example of this would be the use of first and second order thinking. First order thinking is similar to our usual world of objective reality and our cause and effect and modernist problem-solving. In second order thinking, the world is seen through the eye changed by the magic ointment, we can see the world as no longer linear and purely objective, but more dynamic and complex and partially created and constructed by the observer. Looking through the imaginal eye in a clinical context can open to the possibility of working in ways that are non-linear and includes the body and nature, as well as stories, images, and patterns.

Working with the imaginal or creatural in mind, second order thinking can open up to more than just patterns within *language* in the clinical setting, and can be expanded to include much of the symbolic communication and imagery that is usually thought of as confined to psychodynamic or psychoanalytic practice. By reading Bateson in this way the transgressive nature of these images and patterns can allow us to break down some of the boundaries between separate and siloed therapeutic disciplines. Looking through the imaginal eye we begin to look into the world of dreams, body movements, stories and myths, as well as the other-than-human intersubjective encounters in nature, imaginary friends, and psychotic voices, and acknowledge that these could be, like the shapes of animals and plants, "transforms of messages" (Bateson, 1979, p. 17). They are potential communications from the subjugated *fairy world* of the imaginal, communicating information and signals about the patterning of underlying mental processes that we can learn to read by using the hermeneutic skill of imaginal sign reading.

Gardeners who work closely with plants sometimes have an intuitive skill in the art of reading complex signs, through observing and understanding the emergent cycles of plant growth. This way of working with nature is an example of the development of the unconscious skill of hermeneutics. Through understanding the emergent cycles of plant growth, the influences of context and environment, gardeners learn when to watch and wait and when to intervene. Observing plant growth provides a wonderful example of the patterns in healthy systemic development. This skill is essential when working ecopsychologically with children and adolescents, in order to avoid becoming overly prescriptive, or alternately, missing important developmental opportunities.

After seed germination, plants produce their leaves by drawing food and energy from the surrounding environment by combining water, minerals, air, and sunlight to build their physical structure. The growth of the leafy part of the plant, prior to flowering, has useful comparisons with the stage of preadolescent latency period, where both the leaves and preadolescent children are deeply influenced physically by their environment and do not express any outward signs of sexual maturity.

At a certain point in plant growth, just before flowering, this process of producing leaves changes, leaf size begins to reduce, and the plant orientates its growth towards the production of a flower. While it is possible to identify plants from their leaves alone, botanists identify plants definitively by their flowers; the flower is the expression of the plants essential identity, an expression of its *daimon*. This flowering process seems to have an inner urgency towards manifestation and an impulse, a gravitational pull towards sexual reproduction by pollination, and the quality of this urgency is not seen in the leaf growth process. Removal of the flowers, a process known to gardeners as dead heading, does nothing to reduce the urgency of the impulse to flowering in any way, but only encourages more flowers of identical form, although they tend to get smaller and smaller in size.

The study of processes such as plant growth in nature can be helpful for developing hermeneutic skills. Careful observation of patterns in the maturation of flowering plants can provide clues to how to read emergent and fractal expressions of the adolescent *daimon*. It is possible to see flowering in plants as an isomorphic process to the adolescent expression of identity. Just as the size of the flower is dependent on early healthy leaf growth and a nourishing environment, a rich and varied early psychological support in children's lives leads to a strong and healthy adolescence identity.

Though these processes in the growth of plants could be thought of simply as interesting metaphors for human development, seen from an ecopsychological perspective they are more than just similar looking patterns; they share an imaginal depth and deeper study of the comparisons that reveal ever more complex transferable insights into both botany and psychological development. Thinking about these comparisons from the perspective of evolutionary biology, the process of flowering plants and adolescent psychological maturation are completely unconnected. But from an ecopsychological perspective they could be seen as manifestations of the same imaginal impulse, two separate floating icebergs, but connected underwater by a vast body of submerged creatural ice.

Thinking of children and adolescents in this way, we are more likely to hold a respectful position of curiosity and not-knowing (Cecchin, 1987), and embrace the idea of each child as a potential and unique change agents, with the possibility of making a valuable and significant difference within our society. In this way we might begin to formulate a systemic developmental pathway into the future that is not driven top down by a human information culture determined by the past events, but instead draws us forward into emergent new patterns of education and therapeutic support.

Developing a systemic ecopsychological care plan

In order to think about human development from a soul or eco-centric perspective, Bill Plotkin suggests we need to move beyond the limitations of the familiar Western psychological *egocentric* models of human development, where the goal is to re-establish socially acceptable behaviours within WEIRD culture and the focus is on repairing " ... fences of excessive safely, false security, and shallow notions of 'happiness'" (Plotkin, 2013, p. 3). Working with Plotkin's eight stage Soulcentric/ Ecocentric Developmental Wheel and informed by The Circle of Courage and The Four Shields, it is possible to create a different emergent imaginal narrative of healthy human development. These nature based developmental wheels, like the seasons, are non-linear and qualitative, they spiral, rather than cycle. The cycle is never complete but each turn of the wheel digs a little deeper into the fertile soil of imaginal metaphors and the influence of the gravitational pull of the qualities of the four direction of the wheel.

The qualities of Belonging, Mastery, Independence, and Generosity from The Circle of Courage, therefore correspond with the biosocial needs for Attachment, Achievement, Autonomy, and Altruism. They provide four quadrants of different imaginal qualities to arouse curiosity in the formulation of ecopsychological education, and therapeutic care plans.

Attachment

The importance of working to establish a sense of belonging and a secure early attachment in life, is based on the work of Bowlby and Ainsworth, and the understating that these early patterns of relating can continue unconsciously into adult life. Although the brain is developmentally much more open to influences in early life, we know from the study of neuroplasticity that it is possible for these habits to change at any age, although this requires more work the older the brain and the longer these neural pathways have been established. This notion of being able to change unhelpful behaviour gives a rationale for creating supportive and nurturing trauma informed environments for children and young people who have experienced poor or insecure attachment in early life. Brendtro, Mitchel, and McCall, (2009) indicate the importance of building a supportive attachment container using a multi-systemic approach. This work is enhanced by ensuring there are positive role models within a young person's life; parents, teachers, and staff teams but also within organizational team leadership and management structures. This helps to prevent hidden institutional trauma impacting young people and is especially important in cases where the goal of this work is to re-engage young peoples relationships with education, health care, or in healthy home environments.

The nature based model of *The Circle of Courage* suggests that re-establishing the status quo is often not enough, and challenges this view as a reflection of "naïve theories of human behavior" based on seeing challenging behaviour as simply deviant from a socially constructed norm (Brendtro, Brokenleg, & Van Brockern, 1990, p. 20). This means that children are often exposed to the powerful implicit destructive contexts of hopelessness, meaningless work, and loss of a deep sense of belonging, which are widespread in WEIRD culture and these are not acknowledged where the focus is purely on behaviour.

This stage of *learning to belong* corresponds to Plotkin's wheel with stage one and two. Stage one; *The Innocent in the nest*, recognises the need for ego formation and the care of innocence and stage two *the explorer in the garden*, includes the discovery of the natural world and cultural learning. Expanding the idea of multi-agency working to include Plotkin's Soulcentric perspectives, and teaching from The Circle of Courage can help establish a deeper sense of belonging, which is more closely aligned with the experience of preindustrial indigenous cultures (Brendtro, Brokenleg, & Van Brockern, 1990). This view widens the context of attachment to include a strong nested hierarchy of attachment contexts or containers that include parents, extended family, tribal group, and ecological and environmental contexts as concentric support systems of wellbeing.

In pre-industrial cultures it was almost impossible to escape these natural support systems and although today we might consider this way of living to be too socially restrictive, it provided a strong sense of personal and ecological belonging within which young people could grow up. This deeper sense of belonging was reinforced through the use of imaginal and creatural stories, myth, and nature based seasonal rituals, which spoke directly to the non-cognitive part of the brain, serving to reinforce a sense of belonging at a deep psychological level. The breakdown of these ancient indigenous systems of psychological nurture, loss of connection with the land, the breaking of the tribe and deconstruction of extended families, has allowed for an increase in personal ego freedom that is currently enjoyed in the WEIRD world.

Nevertheless, as the remaining indigenous people continually show us, these losses can also result in social break down, domestic violence, alienation, and drug and alcohol abuse, along with uncontrolled environmental destruction that is now prevalent in much of WEIRD culture. When working with young people whose destructive behaviour is driven by attachment difficulties, it is very helpful to build cultural systems around them that understand and support *deep brain learning* and so allow the healing of neurodevelopmental processes that can re-establish a deeper embodied sense of belonging (Brendtro, Mitchel, & McCall, 2009).

Although education systems are socially constructed from the *top down* through our cognitive focused and hierarchal learning structures, from primary to higher education, the natural development of the brain is actually a *bottom up* process (Pankseep, Asma, Curran, Gabriel, & Greif, 2011). This model of the brain is a system of nested brain/mind hierarchies, and although the higher cognitive functions can sometimes regulate primary instincts, it is usually the raw emotional *action systems* of the subcortical region of the brain that are more influential in directing our executive functioning and thinking (Pankseep, Asma, Curran, Gabriel, & Greif, 2011). Seeing the brain this way shows the importance of working with unconscious sensory and motor experiences, and body based emotions for understanding and treating social and psychiatric disorders (Pankseep, Asma, Curran, Gabriel, & Greif, 2011). Pankseep, in his study of the ancient subcortical emotions in the brain of animals discovered seven emotional networks that generate *intentions in action* that operate independently, mostly outside of conscious cortical control. He identified these networks as: seeking, rage, fear, lust, care, grief, and play (Armstrong, 2015).

Using imaginal communication and experiences that include the use of stories and body movement, it is possible to open a dialogue with this part of the brain without needing to use verbal language. Brendtro, Mitchel, and McCall, (2009) describe the importance of carers and teachers building the skills that can reach through the reluctant relationship barrier by earning trust. Where young people have lost the trust of adults it is essential to rebuild a positive alliance in order to engage with them, this is sometimes a difficult process in schools or clinical settings. Using indications from the Plotkin's wheel and Pankseep's work, the action systems of *care* and *play* provides clues to formulations of helpful interventions.

Young people with disrupted patterns of attachment feel safer in non-pressurized and non-structured situations where they are allowed to play. They often feel safer in settings that would have been common in pre-industrial cultures such as: being outside; sitting around a fire, or cooking, eating, and sharing food; having contact with and caring for animals; and can talk more easily while walking or engaged in simple activities and non-directed play. The re-establishment of this deep sense of belonging requires slow and persistent commitment and non-judgmental support from adults and is often a long-term process that can be a real test of relational endurance for the adults concerned.

Achievement

In the same way we observe the turning of the seasons and the growth of plants from leaves, to flowers, to seeds, achieving a sense of belonging leads to the second stage of The Circle of Courage of Mastery or Achievement. This stage of learning to master the inner and outer world corresponds to Plotkin's stages three and four of middle childhood and early adolescence. Stage three *The Thespian at the Oasis*, is involved with the search for a secure authentic sense of self and stage four, *The Wanderer in the Cocoon*, the task of leaving home to follow the call into the underworld depths of adolescent soul searching.

Young people who have experienced early trauma can often move through these states of attachment and achievement too quickly, which can lead to a type of pseudo-adulthood that lacks maturity, characterized by a reluctance to be self-reflective. Like the flowering stage of the plants, this stage of achievement can have a poignant sense of urgency that can be observed in adolescents, as they feel the innocence and security of childhood slipping away. During this phase, adolescents carefully observe and copy social skills they see in the adults around them; like a thespian or actor they try out different identities in a desperate attempt to recreate the lost certainty of childhood, anyway they can. Plotkin captures this process in his descriptions of the stages with the image of the lush abundance and security of the garden of childhood having been reduced to an oasis in the desert;

by adolescence the nurturing water of childhood attachment opportunities has begun to dry up.

Neglect or trauma often results in a characteristic disruption in social development for adolescents if they move through the stage of belonging too quickly, lacking innocence, they have a poor sense of belonging to anything. In fact, they find it difficult to engage in the cognitive possessing of conventional education or the self-regulation and reflection required for talking therapy. Any attempt at moving beyond these hyper-vigilant states is often thwarted by the triggering of the amygdala's autonomic threat response, leading to spontaneous aggression and anger, or dissociation and zoning out. With careful reflective therapeutic work in a non-traumatizing setting it is sometimes possible to widen this window of tolerance to fear and increase the emotional resilience necessary for re-engaging in education or psychotherapy.

Van der Kolk (2014) applied these ideas to his clinical practice and is an advocate for a *bottom up* approach when dealing with young people suffering from developmental trauma and PTSD, and who have become dissociated from their body based feelings. He recommends the value of Eye Movement Desensitization and Reprocessing therapy (EMDR), but also the importance of mindful movement, such as art, music, drama, and yoga.

He explains that these symptoms of developmental trauma underlie different categories of diagnosis, such as ADD and ADHD, and result in many of the behavioural difficulties experienced by professionals who work with children and adolescents in schools, families, mental health setting, foster placements, and detention centres. Adolescents who have experienced early trauma can miss valuable opportunities to learn, and to internalize a locus of control, leading to youth cultures of passive compliance or rebellion to adult values; a learnt irresponsibility (Brendtro, Mitchel, & McCall, 2009).

One very effective way of working with adolescents who are unable to work cognitively or reflectively, is to create physical activities in a safe setting, that are attractive and engaging to the subcortical parts of the brain. The emotion of anger can be very common for adolescents who have experienced life trauma such as domestic violence, and this is understandably very destructive in education settings. Anger or rage and panic or grief are implicit *intention in action* forces in the brain that are often the root of challenging behaviours (Armstrong, 2015; Pankseep, Asma, Curran, Gabriel, & Greif, 2011). Research shows that, strong emotional trauma is not stored explicitly in our memory as information, becomes unconscious implicit memory stored as patterns of embodied experience in the body (Crittenden, 2008; Van der Kolk, 2014). Trauma expert Peter Levine believes that the helpful explicit conscious understanding of traumatic events cannot be formed until the implicit memory patterns have been processed through the body (Armstrong, 2015, p. 154). It is possible to observe the somatized emotions in therapy sessions, particularly gross motor muscle tension and upper body tension in the arms and shoulders that is associated with anger, and lower body and leg twitches that is associated with fear and is often a precursor to the client running out of the room (Armstrong, 2015).

The type of trauma known as a *frozen flight response* to danger, where the energy was never fully discharged, can be released through specific movements (Ogden & Minton, 2006). Working with the body has the potential to help process these emotions at the unconscious level of the implicit and this can make it easier for positive breakthrough experiences, without the risk of explosive destructive anger and grief.

Working for many years with adolescents with very complex behavioural needs in a residential college, I was able to observe the effectiveness of therapeutic and educational experiences through engagement with craft and land work curriculum. These primary practical craft activities, such as blacksmithing, woodwork, leatherwork, pottery, and basketwork, allowed young people the chance to encounter the world through the need to play, by engaging in the physical and practical work outdoors in small teaching groups supported by skilled tutors. The externalized discipline of learning to handle materials in a craft process gradually encourages implicit control of emotions such as anger and grief through the successes and failures of their creative artistic and craft endeavours, without these emotions needing to become fully explicit. Rage could sometimes be expressed through hard physical work such as farming, forestry, or simply walking. Through self-directed gross motor activities and working with animals on the farm, these adolescents were helped to externalize nurture and care in ways that did not risk any perceived danger of direct interpersonal human encounters.

However, more complex craft activities can be used to help master finer motor skills and encourage a corresponding sophistication in the mastery of subtler emotions. Working with a dual perspective, with one eye on the integrity of the physical work and the other on the processing of implicit somatic memory, can be a useful way to create emotionally safe therapeutic environments for supporting adolescents with complex behaviour.

Autonomy

Having learnt to achieve a sense of attachment and achievement in the world the next quadrant in the Circle of Courage is *Independence* or *Autonomy*, where young people take the risk to step out on their own and discover what they can really can do without support. This stage involves the opportunity to try out doing something by themselves that they have previously achieved or mastered under instruction from someone else. Plotkin's wheel identifies this period as the stage five and six, *The Apprentice at the Wellspring* and *The Artisan in the Wild Orchard*. In this model these are the stages of emergent adulthood, accessible through the process of systemic change such as a rite of passage from adolescence to adulthood or a soul initiation

Within WEIRD culture adulthood is gained through education; mastering of sufficient skills to be able to step into the workplace and find a role in the world where one can inhabit the skin of a secure social self. In indigenous cultures, where children were encouraged to master adult skills early, this was often achieved prior to the stage of adolescence. However, having mastered the authentic social self, there is a deeper, soul centric story that emerges at adolescence; a impulse to risk old certainties for the wild excitement of leaving home in search of an encounter with a magical otherness in search of the gift of a life purpose.

Mythologists Robert Bly and Martin Shaw describe how these patterns and imaginal narratives in myths and stories have been used as route maps of psychological and spiritual development (Bly, 1990; Shaw, 2011). Likewise, the nature based wheels of Plotkin, and Foster and Little both identify this deeper and richer call to autonomy, not simply as compliance to social and cultural expectations, but as a call to hunt for the well spring of our integrity and our gift to the world, a search for the *daimon*. In Joseph Campbell's *Hero's Journey*, this stage is *the call to adventure*, an underworld journey that can result in imaginal transformation. As nature undergoes the season of autumn the human equivalent is the symbolic death of our hard won social identity to find a more authentic sense of self (Campbell, 1993). Plotkin names this stage just prior to soul initiation as *The Wanderer in the Cocoon*, in which the loss of childlike certainty and a need for change is felt; a gravitational pull to leave the fragile adolescent social identity behind and explore the mysteries of the psychological underworld. Without cultural and psychological road maps of this imaginal journey, the opportunity of this stage of development remains invisible within WEIRD culture and can become instead a depressive acceptance and compliance to a socially constructed culture or an attraction to counter cultures and illegal risk-taking activities readily available in drug and criminal sub cultures.

Rites of passage

However reimagining these challenges in the context of a rite of passage can create different outcomes for young people who present in a clinical or educational setting (White & Epston, 1990, p. 7). An adolescent crisis that manifests as defiance, self-harm, or suicidal ideation, that is characteristic of stage four, *The Wanderer in the Cocoon*, seen from the medical model perspective, might be labelled as a disorder and therefore lead to a formulation of encouraging the re-establishment of a former redundant social self. Reframing this experience using an imaginal understanding of the social ritual process of a rite of passage, could view such a crisis as a marker or signal of the call to deeper psychological self-knowledge. *The Apprentice at the Wellspring*, is a call to authenticity, excitement, and initiation into the search for a deeper purpose of learning to embody soul in our culture (Plotkin, 2008).

According to the Van Gennep model, a rite of passage is part of a ritualized process that has three phases. These are: (1) *severance*, the leaving behind of an identity or status that no longer serves; (2) *liminality* or *the threshold*, a transitional space, of having left the familiar and entering into a stage of not knowing, involving risk and uncertainty; and (3) *incorporation* and the beginning of the phase of taking on a new role or identity, which is then recognized by the community (White & Epston, 1990). Nelson Mandela described in his autobiography, how he joined a group of boys and lived away from his village during the process of traditional Xhosa initiation. During the preparation for his circumcision the group lived in the bush in specially built huts, as part of the severance phase before the threshold of the ritual into manhood. After the circumcision the huts were ritually burnt to the ground and Mandela described looking back at the ashes and realizing that his childhood was now completely over (Mandela, 1994, p. 30).

The negative psychological and social impact of the lack of contemporary adolescent rite of passage in WEIRD culture has been well documented by Mahdi, Foster and Little, Somé, and others (Mahdi, Foster, & Little, 1987; Mahdi, Christopher, & Meade 1996; Somé, 1993, 1995). Without a healthy rite of passage the gravitational pull of a psychological threshold experience can be exploited for more destructive ends and has been used in the recruitment, abuse, and training of child soldiers in South Africa, by the ANC and in the training of Islamic child terrorists and suicide bombers.

There is renewed interest in reinstating adolescent rites of passage, often linked to the women's movement and the men's movement and some very beautiful work is being done by groups who support young people through this threshold phase, through camping trips and solo time in wilderness settings, as well as community work. These processes usually borrow to a greater or lesser extent from ingenious models and are most effective where new insights are embodied and become part to implicit memory in the same way we learn a new skill.

Systemic thinking can provide further insight to why rites of passage are important for adolescents, particularly if a rite of passage is formulated as a *systemic phase change*. Since systemic phase change is triggered by changes in complexity, such as the freezing of water to ice, or the change from leaf to flower in plants, and requires a process of break down and rebuilding, it resembles the symbolic death and rebirth that we see in many mythic stories. The outcome of systemic change is emergent and unpredictable, but has the potential to bring about something completely different and new. Healthy rites of passage therefore have the potential to bring about emergent perspectives within communities who engage with them, so that initiated adolescents and adults have the potential to become the change agents for their communities.

If Bateson is right, and mind and nature are both subsets of creatura, a self-healing imaginal matrix, then any exposure to nature that is unrestricted by linear formulations is likely to increase complexity in both systems of nature and the psyche or soul and the possibility of a spontaneous reorganizing phase change can occur. The successful negotiation of systemic change in adolescents can therefore be supported by open access to ecologically healthy land where they are exposed to new creatural and imaginal information patterns in nature.

This process needs the support of a community of experienced elders, who have ecological knowledge of the land as well a good psychological understanding of adolescent psycho-spiritual development, along with a "language" to navigate in the imaginal or creatural world. This community then has the potential to provide the physical and psychological safety systems to support contemporary rites of passage for adolescents through such experiences as; solo time in nature, or wilderness experiences, and vision fasts.

Altruism

The fourth stage in The Circle of Courage is *Generosity* or *Altruism* and corresponds in The Four Shields model to the North Shield of *generative adulthood*. This is highly valued as a time of giving back to society, not just in providing material wealth, but also in facilitating and supporting the healthy growth of the next generation. In Plotkin's Soulcentric model he identifies these two stages as, *The Master in the Grove of Elders*, that involves caring for the soul of the more-than-human community; and *The Sage in the Mountain Cave*, which includes tending the universe with the gift of grace. These are imaginal, not literal images of the adult work that become possible after soul initiation and the discovery of a personal wellspring of inspiration to guide our adult life. This stage of the nature based wheel can provide a possible template for healthy work places and communities, where adults can support child and adolescence development from a position which is both ecologically and psychologically informed and guided by a self-healing imaginal narrative that connects nature and the human soul.

Conclusion

Taking the long view of human development that includes the whole of our indigenous history can open a new way to see the world, and break through the social constructed boundaries of the medical or mechanistic perspective. This way of learning to recognize the imaginal and creatural aspects of the world opens up the possibility of working with nature and the human mind in a way that is more ecological and systemic. An imaginal perspective provides a rationale for the use of nature based developmental wheels that offer a completely different quality of mental health development that can complement contemporary perspectives. The use of nature based developmental tools helps focus curiosity on the quality of underlying attachment patterns, the integration and mastery of the body and the threshold experience of systemic phase change or soul encounter. This nature based perspective also invites us to build cultures where adults embrace developmental elderhood, through the process of initiation and subsequent integration of their life experiences, enabling them to support children and adolescence. The next task seems to me to be the mastery of imaginal and creatural perspectives, as described by Bateson and Corbin, which provides insight into how the systems of nature and the human mind work together and bring this understanding into mainstream WEIRD culture.

Embracing a systemic ecopsychological view of human development along side professional training allows for a new narrative of how human beings and nature are connected. This challenges the WEIRD cultural tyranny of directed thinking that cannot recognize the subtlety of the unity between mind and nature, so unconsciously perpetrates, and perpetuates patterns of behaviour that are unhealthy and destructive to both nature and the human soul. This book is an invitation to join the 'terrible and beautiful' dance between nature and the indigenous mind (Bateson, 1979, p. 8).

Epilogue

I will leave the epilogue to the thirteenth century Persian poet Jalāl ad-Dīn Muhammad Rūmī, a master of describing imaginal narratives of our relationship between the human soul and the world. In this poem he brings curiosity and gentleness to a description of the threshold between the certainty of the cognitively known and the ephemeral experience of fully encountering the world of nature.

Story Water

A story is like water
That you heat for your bath.
It takes messages between the fire and your skin. It lets them meet,
and it cleans you!

Very few can sit down
in the middle of the fire itself,
like a salamander, or Abraham.
We need intermediaries.

A feeling of fullness comes,
but usually it takes some bread
to bring it.

Beauty surrounds us,
but usually we need to be walking
in a garden to know it.

The body itself is a screen
to shield and partially reveal
the light blazing
inside your presence.

Water, stories, the body,
all the things we do, are mediums
that hide and show what's hidden.

Study them,
and enjoy this being washed
with a secret we sometimes know,
and then not.

(Barks, 1995 p. 171)

References

Abrams, D. (1996). *The Spell of the Sensuous*. New York, NY: Pantheon Books.

Alexander, B. (2001). *The Roots of Addiction in the Free Market Society*. Canadian Center for Policy Alternatives. Available at http://www.cfdp.ca/roots.pdf [Last accessed 5 December 2017].

American Psychiatric Association (APA). (1952). *Diagnostic and Statistical Manual of Mental Disorders,* 5th edition. Washington, DC: American Psychiatric Association.

Armstrong, C. (2015). *The Therapeutic "Aha!": Strategies for Getting your Client Unstuck*. New York, NY: W. W. Norton & Co.

Atchley, R., Atchley, P., & Strayer, D. (2012). Creativity in the wild: Improving creative reasoning through immersion in natural settings. *PLOS One, 7*: e51474.

Barks, C. (1995). *Rumi Selected Poems*. London: Penguin Books.

Bateson, G. (1979). *Mind and Nature: A Necessary Unity*. London: Wildwood.

Bateson, G., & Bateson, M. C. (2005). *Angels Fear: Towards an Epistemology of the Sacred*. New York, NY: Hampton Press.

Bateson, N. (Dir.). (2010). *An Ecology of Mind – A Daughters Portrait of Gregory Bateson*. www.bullfrogfilms.com

Becvar, D., & Becvar, R. (1999). *First Order Cybernetics: Definitions of Concepts. Systems Theory and Family Therapy: A Primer*. Lanham: University Press of America.

Berger, R. (2006). Using contact with nature, creativity and rituals as a therapeutic medium with children with learning difficulties: a case study. *Emotional and Behavioural Difficulties, 11:* 135–146.

Bettmann, J., Demong, E., & Jasperson, R. (2008). Treating adolescents with adoption and attachment issues in wilderness therapy settings. *Journal of Therapeutic Schools and Programs, 3(1):* 116–137.

Bettmann, J., Russell, K., & Parry, K. (2012). How substance abuse recovery skills, readiness to change and symptom reduction impact change processes in wilderness therapy participants. *Journal of Child and Family Studies, 22:* 1039–1050.

Bettmann, J., Gillis, H., Speelman E., Parry, K., & Case, J. (2016). A meta-analysis of wilderness therapy outcomes for private pay clients. *Journal of Child and Family Studies, 25:* 2659–2673.

Bird, W. (2007). *Natural Thinking: Investigating the Links Between the Natural Environment, Biodiversity and Mental Health*. Royal Society for the Protection of Birds. www.rspb.org.uk/policy/health

Bly, R. (1990). *Iron John: Men and Masculinity*. Boston: Addison–Wesley.

Bortoft, H. (1996). *The Wholeness of Nature: Goethe's Way of Science*. Edinburgh: Floris Books.

Brendtro, L., Brokenleg, M., & Van Brockern, S. (1990). *Reclaiming Youth at Risk: Our Hope for the Future*. Bloomington: National Educational Service.

Brendtro, L., Mitchel, M., & McCall, H. (2009). *Deep Brain Learning: Pathways to Potential with Challenging Youth*. Albion: Starr Commonwealth.

Buhner, S. H. (2014). *Plant Intelligence and the Imaginal Realm*. Rochester: Bear & Co.

Burns, G. W. (2000). When watching a sunset can help a relationship dawn anew: Nature-guided therapy for couples and families. *Australian and New Zealand Journal of Family Therapy, 21*: 184–190.

Campbell, J. (1993). *The Hero with a Thousand Faces*. London: Fontana Press.

Carson, R. (1962). *Silent Spring*. Boston, MA: Houghton Mifflin.

Cecchin, G. (1987). Hypothesizing, circularity, and neutrality revisited: An invitation to curiosity. *Family Process, 26*: 405–413.

Cheetham, T. (2003). *The World Turned Inside Out: Henry Corbin and Islamic Mysticism*. Woodstock: Spring Journal Books.

Cheetham, T. (2015). *Imaginal Love: The Meaning of Imagination in Henry Corbin and James Hillman*. Thompson: Spring Publications.

Crittenden, P. (2008). *Raising Parents: Attachment, Parenting and Child Safety*. Cullompton: Willan Publishing.

Crittenden, P., & Landini, A. (2015). Attachment relationships as semiotic scaffolding systems. *Biosemiotics, 8*: 257–273.

Darwin, C. (1898). *The Power of Movement in Plants*. New York, NY: D. Appleton and company.

Diamond, J. (2012). *The World Until Yesterday*. London: Penguin Books.

Duncan, R. (1993). Touch the earth: An ecology field trip allows students to develop ecological awareness by experiencing wilderness. *Resurgence, 160*: 10–11.

Duncan, R. (2013). *Mind and Nature Revisited: In Search of a Unifying Language and Practice Using Systemic Evaluation*. Bristol: University of Bristol.

Duncan, R. (2014). Soul and nature: The two lost lovers from the land of Tír na nÓg. *European Journal of Ecopsychology, 5*: 64–75.

Ecopsychology Online. (1999). http://isis.csuhayward.edu/ALSS/ECO

Ecker, B., Ticic, R., & Hulley, L. (2011). *Unlocking the Emotional Brain: Eliminating Symptoms at Their Roots Using Memory Reconsolidation*. New York, NY: Routledge.

Freke, T., & Gandy, P. (2002). *The Jesus Mysteries: Was the Original Jesus a Pagan God?* London: Thorsons.

Freuchen, P. (1961). *The Book of the Eskimo*. New York, NY: World Publishing Co.

Foster, S., & Little, M. (1998a). *The Four Shields: The Initiatory Seasons of Human Nature*. Big Pine: Lost Borders Press.

Foster, S., & Little, M. (1998b). *Lost Borders: Coming of Age in the Wilderness*. Big Pine: Lost Borders Press.

Glendenning, C. (1994). *My Name is Chellis and I'm in Recovery from Western Civilization*. Boston: Shambhala.

Greenway, R. (1995). The wilderness effect and ecopsychology. In: T. Roszak, M. Gomes, & A. Kanner (Eds.), *Ecopsychology: Restoring the Earth Healing the Mind*. (pp. 122–135). San Francisco, CA: Sierra Club Books.

Heyerdahl, T. (1976). *Fatu Hiva: Back to Nature*. London: Penguin Books.

Hillman, J. (1997). *The Soul's Code: In Search of Character and Calling*. London: Bantam Books.

Hine, R., Pretty, J., & Barton, J. (2009). *Research Project: Social, Psychological and Cultural Benefits of Large Natural Habitat and Wilderness Experiences: A Review of*

Current Literature for the Wilderness Foundation. Essex: Interdisciplinary Centre for Environment and Society, University of Essex.

Hoag, M., Combs, K., Roberts, S., & Logan, P. (2016). Pushing beyond outcomes: What else changes in wilderness therapy. *Journal of Therapeutic Schools and Programs, 08.01.06*: 46–56.

Hoeller, S. (1982). *The Gnostic Jung: And the Seven Sermons of the Dead.* Wheaton: Quest Books.

Hoffmeyer, J. (2008). *A Legacy for Living Systems: Gregory Bateson as a Precursor to Biosemiotics.* New York, NY: Springer.

Hoffmeyer, J. (2009). *Biosemiotics: An Examination into the Signs of Life and Life of Signs.* Scranton: University of Scranton Press.

Jones, E. (1993). *Family Systems Therapy: Development in the Milan-Systemic Therapies.* New York, NY: John Wiley & Sons.

Jordan, M. (2015). *Nature and Therapy: Understanding Counseling and Psychotherapy in Outdoor Spaces.* London: Routledge.

Kinderman, P., Read, J., Moncrieff, J., & Bentall, R. (2012). Drop the language of disorder. *Evidence-Based Mental Health, 16(1):* 2–3.

Kohner, M. (2012). *The Transformative Function of Symbols: An Exploration Through Wilderness Rites of Passage.* Wright Institute Graduate School of Psychology. Ann Arbor, MI: proQuest.

Kuo, F. E., & Faber, T. A. (2004). The potential natural treatment for attention-deficit hyperactivity disorder: Evidence from a national study. *American Journal of Public Health, 94:* 1580–1586.

Launer, J. (2001). What ever happened to Biology? Reconnecting family therapy with its evolutionary origins. *Journal of Family Therapy, 23:* 155–170.

Levine, P., & Frederic, A. (2012). *Waking the Tiger: Healing Trauma.* Berkley, CA: North Atlantic Press.

Lewontin, R. (2001). *The Triple Helix: Gene, Organism and Environment.* Cambridge, MA: Harvard Press.

Lievegoed, B. (1946). *Phases of Childhood: Growing in Body, Soul and Spirit.* Edinburgh: Floris Press.

Lopez, B. (1986). *Arctic Dreams: Imagination and Desire in a Northern Landscape.* London: Picador.

Lukas, G. (Dir). (1997). *Star Wars.* Hollywood: Lucasfilm Ltd.

Macdonald, H. (2014). *H is for Hawk.* London: Vintage Books.

Macey, J., & Brown, M. (1998). *Coming Back to Life: Practices to Reconnect Our Lives, Our World.* Canada: New Society Publishers.

Mahdi, L. C., Foster, S., & Little, M. (1987). *Betwixt and Between: Patterns of Masculine and Feminine Initiation.* Chicago, IL: Open Court.

Mahdi, L. C., Christopher, N. G., & Meade, M. (1996). *Crossroads: The Quest for Contemporary Rites of Passage.* Chicago, IL: Open Court.

Mandela, N. (1994). *Long Walk to Freedom.* New York, NY: Abacus.

Maslow, A. H. (1971). *The Farther Reaches of Human Nature.* New York, NY: Viking Press.

McGilchrist, I. (2009). *The Master and his Emissary: The Divided Brain and the Making of the Western World.* London: Yale University Press.

McLuhan, T. C. (1971). *Touch the Earth: A Self-Portrait of Indian Existence.* New York, NY: Pocket Books.

Miller, W. (1955). Two concepts of authority. *American Anthropologist, 57*: 271–289.

Monbiot, G. (2013). *Feral: Rewilding the Land, Sea and Human Life*. London: Penguin Books.

Music, G. (2014). *The Good Life: Wellbeing and the Science of Altruism, Selfishness and Immorality*. New York, NY: Routledge.

National Offenders Management Service. (NOMS). (2006). Prison population and accommodation briefing. London: NOMS.

Natural England. (2016). *A Review of Nature-based Interventions for Mental Health Care* [NECR204]. Available at http://publications.naturalengland.org.uk/publication/4513819616346112 [Last accessed 5 December 2017].

Ogden, P., & Minton, K. (2006). *Trauma and the Body: A Sensorimotor Approach to Psychotherapy*. New York, NY: Norton.

Panksepp, J., Asma, S., Curran, G., Gabriel, R., & Greif, T. (2011). The philosophical implications of affective neuroscience. *Journal of Consciousness Studies, 19:* 6–28.

Park, B. J., Tsunetsugu, Y., Kasetani, T., Hirano, H., Kagawa, T., Sato, M., & Miyazaki, Y. (2007). Physiological effects of Shinrin-yoku (taking in the atmosphere of the forest) – using salivary cortisol and cerebral activity as indicators. *Journal of Physiological Anthropology, 26:* 123–128.

Peacock, J., Hines, R., & Pretty, J. (2008). *Wilderness Therapy: The TurnAround 2007 Project*. Essex: University of Essex.

Pinnock, D., & Douglas-Hamilton, D. (1997). *Gang Rituals and Rites of Passage*. Cape Town: Africa Sun Press.

Plotkin, B. (2003). *Soulcraft: Crossing into the Mysteries of Nature and Psyche*. Novato: New World Library.

Plotkin, B. (2008). *Nature and the Human Soul: Cultivating Wholeness in a Fragmented World*. Novato: New World Library.

Plotkin, B. (2013). *Wild Mind: A Field Guide to the Human Psyche*. Novato: New World Library.

Rivet, M., & Street, E. (2009). *Family Therapy: 100 Key Points and Techniques*. New York, NY: Routledge.

Romanyshyn, R. D. (1999). *The Soul in Grief: Love, Death and Transformation*. Berkeley, CA: North Atlantic Books.

Romanyshyn, R. D. (2007). *The Wounded Researcher: Research with Soul in Mind*. New Orleans, LA: Spring Journal Publications.

Roszak, T. (1992). *The Voice of the Earth: An Exploration of Ecopsychology*. New York, NY: Simon & Schuster.

Russell, K. C., Hendee, J., & Phillips-Miller, D. (1999). *How Wilderness Therapy Works: An Examination of the Wildness Therapy Process to Treat Adolescents with Behavior Problems and Addictions*. Outdoor Behavioral Healthcare. Available at: https://obhcouncil.com/wp-content/uploads/2012/02/article2.pdf [Last accessed 5 December 2017].

Sahtouris, E. (2000). *Earth Dance: Living Systems in Evolution*. Lincoln, NE: iUniverse.

Sardello, R. (2008). *Love and the Soul: Creating a Future for the Earth*. Berkeley, CA: New Atlantic Books.

Schad, W. (1977). *Man and Mammals: Toward a Biology of Form*. Grapevine: Waldorf Press.

Selvini-Palazzoli, M., Boscolo, L., Cecchin, G., & Prata, G. (1980). Hypothesizing – circularity – neutrality: Three guidelines for the conductor of the session. *Family Process, 19(1):* 3–12.

Shaw, M. (2011). *A Branch from the Lightning Tree: Ecstatic Myth and the Grace in Wildness*. Oregon, OR: White Cloud Press.

Sheldrake, R. (2012). *Science Set Free: 10 Paths to New Discovery*. New York, NY: Crown Publishing.

Shepard, P. (1982). *Nature and Madness*. San Francisco, SA: Sierra Club Books.

Shepard, P. (1998). *Coming Home to the Pleistocene*. Washington, DC: Island Press.

Siegel, D. J. (2017). *Mind: A Journey to the Heart of Being Human*. New York, NY: W. W. Norton & Co.

Somé, M. P. (1993). *Ritual: Power, Healing and Community*. Portland, OR: Swan/Raven & Co.

Somé, M. P. (1995). *Of Water and the Spirit: Ritual, Magic and Initiation in the Life of an African Shaman*. New York, NY: Penguin Books.

Steiner, R. (2000). *Nature's Open Secret: Introductions to Goethe's Scientific Writings*. New York, NY: Anthroposophic Press.

Suchantke, A. (2009). *Metamorphosis: Evolution in Action*. New York, NY: Adonis Press.

Suchantke, A. (2001). *Eco-geography: What We See When We Look at Landscapes*. Great Barrington: Lindisfarne Books.

Tomlinson, R. (2011). Good from woods case studies. Available at: www.goodfromwoods.co.uk/case-studies-2/

Totton, N. (2011). *Wild Therapy: Undomesticating Inner and Outer Worlds*. Ross-on-Wye: PCCS Books.

Ulrich, R. (1983). Aesthetic and affective response to natural environment. In: I. Atman & J. F. Wohlwill (Eds.), *Human Behaviour and the Natural Environment* (pp. 85–126). New York, NY: Plenum.

Van der Kolk, B. (2014). *The Body Keeps the Score: Brain, Mind and the Body in the Healing of Trauma*. New York, NY: Viking Books.

Van Evera-Roth, L. G. (2002). *Meaningful Rites: A Passage into Life Purpose Through Education*. MA: Sonoma State University.

Van Gennep, A. (1961). *The Rites of Passage*. Chicago: University of Chicago Press.

White, M., & Epston, D. (1990). *Narrative Means to Therapeutic Ends*. New York, NY: W. W. Norton & Co.

Wilderness Foundation. (2009). Umzi Wethu – Nature, nurture, future [video]. Available at: www.youtube.com/watch?v=1hALwxwzlFU [Last accessed 5 December 2017].

Willis, A. (2011). Re-storying wilderness and adventure therapies: Healing places and selves in an era of environmental crisis. *Journal of Adventure Education and Outdoor Learning, 11:* 91–108.

Wilson, E. O. (1984). *Biophilia: The Human Bond with Other Species*. Cambridge, MA: Harvard University Press.

Wood, C., Braggs, R., Pretty, J., & Barton, J. (2012). *The Turnaround Project – Phase 3 Project for the Wilderness Foundation*. Essex: University of Essex.

Zimmerman, J., & Coyle, V. (1996). *The Way of Council*. Las Vegas: Bramble Books.

Zohar, D. (1990). *The Quantum Self: Human Nature and Consciousness Defined by the New Physics*. New York, NY: William Morrow.

Index

29 30   Deleuze

6 7   6th Playback

13 14   Deleuze

20 21   19–21 Dramaturgy

27 28   27–28 wildwomen